DINNER
AT THE
LONG TABLE

ANDREW TARLOW & ANNA DUNN
WITH SCARLETT LINDEMAN

INTRODUCTION BY KATE HULING

PHOTOGRAPHS BY MICHAEL GRAYDON & NIKOLE HERRIOTT

ART DIRECTION BY BECKY JOHNSON

TEN SPEED PRESS
Berkeley

*You are the music
while the music lasts*

—T. S. Eliot

DINNER AT THE LONG TABLE

EAT
SUNSHINE

read

don't follow recipes

be the whale

roast a goat

breathe fire

return to the cave

cook with fire

use wild herbs

talk to ghosts

get things from the sea

lacto-ferment

preserve ingredients

save the seasons

make vinegar

participate in the timeless

have a point of view

fail at aioli

clean squid

manage the alien

learn to improvise

read *Moby-Dick*

never measure

variations on a theme

taste your food

cook for days

stop making sense

eat for weeks

cooking as a thing to do

pass the time

make drinks

light the candles

magic

spend your life thinking about dinner

bathe in olive oil

take care of strangers

who is a stranger

we all survive on the same things

beans hold a purpose

water

fire

earth

boil everything

the dark heart of the artichoke

burn the corn

turn the clocks back

turn the clocks around

what is for lunch

drink wine

wine as a companion

fermented fruit juice

journey into the night

journey into might

search for food

drink Chartreuse

raw eggs

remember the mortar

liquor, spirit fairies, spirits in the night

game changers

clean your plate, share your plate, everyone eats out of the same bowl

cook what you can eat

compost

put it back into the ground

dust to dust

know the golden rule

are you hungry yet

remember what you forgot

the only challenge is time

don't buy food from strangers

drink cans of beer with Guy Jones

make friends

you are not alone

just keep reading

cook with clay

visit the mountains and eat there

food tastes better in the wild

food tastes better when it's wild

type with your fingers

eat with your fingers

speak in metaphors

salt on the flames

and if you don't know

look at books

now you know

failure is a fine option

take risks

cook it until you understand

make a cookbook you can read and carry it with you

make something that can last

get better at cooking

feed your new friends

set off the smoke alarm

the fire department should knock on your door

always offer them a book

never flour on the flames

build a fire

cook on cast iron

use good pots

cook with color

set the table

get your hands dirty

clean your kitchen

sharpen knives

carbon steel

make a list of books to write

use wooden spoons

always write a menu

write a menu for every meal, even the small ones

find a butcher

buy food for the day not the week

glug glug

eat the photo shoot

choose your own adventure

have a pantry

or don't

feed your cat the bones

eat oysters at home

make a journal

make a cookbook

have a dance party after dinner

you need balloons

carry the spices home in your pockets

draw the goat

bitter is ok

write about it until you understand it

know what keeps

listen to the music your friends make

don't lose the plot

go to Saltie

always aioli

cook Thanksgiving twice a year

there's always a motive

one bad knife

make a movie

set the table

share your chair

show your toes

ask for writing

always, to the ocean

look for the comma

make lists

build a table

eat on the floor

invite kids in

roll up your sleeves

help her roll up her sleeves

wear aprons

cook with wood

cook barefoot

meet your farmer

cook for them

eat small fish

make stock

run-on sentences

write a book without writing a sentence

find your heroes

marinate olives

live like a hero

cook to keep the house warm

always a salad

eat on benches

eat with spoons

put your plate on your knee

you are never done

stay fluid

make a condiment

cook for tomorrow

how do you end

paint the clock

EGGS ALL DAY

AN INTRODUCTION
Kate Huling

I met Andrew in 1998 at the Odeon, in Tribeca. I was twenty and a new waitress and Andrew was twenty-eight and the senior bartender with a bad attitude and I was crazy for him from minute one. After a month of cheeky banter and snarky flirting, he asked me to come over to his house so that he could cook for me. I put on my red sparkly trousers as a good luck charm and got on the J train to Brooklyn. It was my first trip over the Williamsburg Bridge, and when I got to the other side and walked down the metal staircase, he was there waiting for me, and he kissed me for the first time on the cheek.

He had already bought a skirt steak from Gourmet Garage in the city, and we went into the Korean produce market on Broadway and bought zucchini and cilantro and salad greens. Andrew had built out a six-thousand-square-foot loft on Broadway with his roommates Mark Firth and Martin Cohen. Martin was a mosaicist, and his tile work was all over the open bathrooms. Andrew's paintings were hung on all of the walls. There were great windows looking out at the bridge and Manhattan, and there was a bathtub in the middle of the living area.

Andrew made a cilantro pesto, marinated the skirt steak, tossed the zucchini with peperoncini, and then packed everything up and we climbed out the door onto the roof. He grilled the steak and the zucchini and made a salad, and then everyone started coming onto the roof. Martin and Mark and Sasha and South African Mark. We all sat around an old wooden door propped up on sawhorses and ate and watched the sun set over the city. It was Bastille Day 1998.

Mark and Andrew had just signed the lease for the Diner, and I hadn't really spent much time with Mark. I could chart his comings and goings by the presence or absence of stilettos outside his bedroom door, but otherwise, we only saw him when we went to visit him at Balthazar, where he was bartending. I was curious about why Andrew had chosen this reckless Don Juan for a business partner, not knowing that he would very soon become one of my most favorite people.

They had just gotten the keys to the 1920s Pullman dining car on the corner of Broadway and Berry in Williamsburg. I would have followed Andrew to the ends of the earth, so if he was digging out the layer of fat-cured cockroaches under the dining car's bar and demoing the kitchen, then that is what I wanted to do, too. We spent that summer covered in sweat, grease, and construction dust, so much so that Andrew made a habit of taking an afternoon swim in the East River in his underwear.

After the demo was done, Andrew, Mark, and their friends Ken Reynolds and Eoin Kileen got to work with the tiling, plumbing, woodworking, and electrical, and even though I was still in college I didn't have much to do. There was nowhere for them to eat lunch on the south side of Williamsburg, so I spent my mornings before class making food for the crew. I hadn't really done much cooking, so I enjoyed teaching myself how to make bread and pastas and roast chickens with Andrew's copies of the *River Café* cookbooks, and they all enjoyed taking a break and coming home to a big lunch.

As winter approached, it was time to find a chef. I think that it is important to say that Andrew and Mark opened Diner because they wanted a place to eat and hang out, not because they wanted to own a restaurant. They sketched out menus with eggs all day, tuna fish sandwiches, bangers and mash, roast chicken, and pressed cheese sandwiches. They imagined a long line of bridge construction workers eating egg sandwiches at the bar, with themselves sitting at Table 1, playing backgammon and eating ham and cheese. What defines Diner and the food of all of our restaurants today is that stroke of magic that convinced Caroline Fidanza to be our chef after one dinner out with Andrew and Mark. She didn't know us, and we had never tried her food.

Caroline had left her post as sous chef for Peter Hoffman at Savoy, and while soul-searching about her next move, she was making the desserts at Teddy's on the north side of the neighborhood. Maybe it was the kind of freedom that Andrew and Mark offered her that made her put her apron back on and become our chef. Maybe it was Andrew's drive or Mark's sense of humor. She signed on, and then we didn't even sit down to cook together or talk about menus. The next time we saw her was when she and I painted the floor of the walk-in refrigerator just days before opening.

On December 31, 1998, we didn't have gas yet or an exhaust, but we knew we needed to get the doors open. Caroline and her sister Jackie arrived at the loft with a giant cassoulet pot, beans, sausages, and confit duck legs, and she prepared the most important meal of our lives, for all of the people who had worked for six months, mostly without pay, to build Diner. There were more than twenty of us and we sat at a very long table in the back room at Diner. Andrew, Mark, and I were at one end of the table. I watched Mark and Andrew take their first bites of Caroline's cassoulet and look at each other as if they had just won the lottery. It will forever be one of my fondest memories. They hadn't any idea of the caliber of the person, and chef, they had found to run their kitchen. In that moment, it became crystal clear that she could make anything happen for them.

Caroline had made a giant watercress salad to go with the cassoulet, which was followed by large slices of manchego cheese and quince paste, and then a rum chocolate cake, though we were too full to eat it. We still didn't know Caroline back on that freezing cold night, but after the crowds of people packed the Diner and South African Mark was blasting Radiohead and Jamiroquai and all of our guests were drunk from too many cosmopolitans and metropolitans, Andrew, Mark, and I found ourselves in the kitchen with Caroline, eating the chocolate cake with forks right off the platter. Our lifelong love affair with her began.

ORIGINAL DINER MENU FROM JANUARY 1999

```
Greek Salad (chopped romaine and herbs)

Beet Salad (greens with grated raw beets and feta cheese)

Goat Cheese Salad (greens with marinated goat cheese,
roasted squash, and walnuts)

Roast Chicken with Mash

Hanger Steak with Mash

Rib Eye with Fries

Burger with Fries

Chocolate Cake with Whipped Cream
```

Every day after that first day, we woke up at 6 a.m. for garbage pickup and to receive the fish. By day, we worked in the kitchen with Caroline to help her prep. Then at 4 p.m. Andrew, Mark, and I ran down the street to take showers and came back to work the front of the house—Mark behind the bar and Andrew and me on the floor. We didn't print out menus. Our menu was recited to the customers and written on the butcher paper of each table so that they could remember it. Caroline quickly felt comfortable running the menu and started making the specials that became the core of Diner's offerings. Her list of specials grew, and the food on the regular menu dwindled.

What we learned very quickly was that the core of Caroline's cooking is her frugality. She bought local bluefish and mackerel because it was good and cheap. She went to the farmers' market instead of ordering from food purveyors because it was better and cheaper; she didn't garnish and she made her own crème fraîche and mayonnaise for the same reason. In most cases, plates only had three or four elements. There is a security about her food and what is good. That is how she defines a plate: by whether it's good or not, whether it is in service of the ingredients as well as the season, not whether it will impress you.

Her biggest challenge in the early days was that it was impossible to find hardworking, dedicated support in the kitchen. She felt that all of the talent was in Manhattan and that no one wanted to work in our shitty seventy-year-old Diner car underneath the Williamsburg Bridge. So much so that Andrew, Mark, and I continued to have weekly kitchen shifts. I sent out overdressed salads all night, while Mark and Andrew, with blue side towels wrapped around their heads, ditched their garde-manger duties and tried to weasel themselves onto the grill station.

It felt like the Wild West on Broadway in those days. We could do whatever we wanted. If we had a long wait for the outdoor tables, we would just keep adding more of them down Broadway toward the East River. We built a tented room, back behind the dumpsters, with a poorly designed open fireplace and very illegally cooked Sunday dinners, with Caroline and me running a small menu that we had written. It was so smoky back there that we, along with the customers, would finish the night with red eyes and deep coughs, but somehow we still have fond memories of those dinners with overdressed salads (my specialty), crostini, grilled pizzas, and whole fish.

Andrew and I were working hard in those years and didn't do much cooking, eating, or living outside of the Diner, until I got pregnant in 2000 with Elijah. There was still smoking in restaurants, and the Diner dinner service took place in a cloud of smoke from start to finish. Andrew and I stopped cooking in the kitchen and closing the place at 3 a.m. and hired a couple of people. We started cooking and entertaining at home again. We also got to hang out with Caroline outside of work, which was a revelation.

One night she invited the whole staff over to her house for sauce. We arrived in her Greenpoint apartment to bowls of rigatoni with meatballs, spicy sausage, rich meaty tomato sauce, and a spoonful of ricotta cheese. We all sat on the floor and ate first and then second helpings of the food that she would typically make with her family in Poughkeepsie, New York. Being in her house that night, we all got to see a different side of Caroline, the one that loved cooking and wasn't overwhelmed by her weak kitchen staff and the pressure that Andrew always put on her to do more. This was a night that taught us how important it is to cook for and with everyone beyond the confines of the restaurant.

Elijah was due in the spring of 2001. Inspired by a Greek Easter Meal, the day before his due date I decided that if I cooked a sacrificial lamb over an open fire, Elijah's birth would come the next day as planned. Mark and I drove around the city buying the leg of lamb, snap peas, artichokes, potatoes, and large rosemary fronds for basting. We followed Lulu Peyraud's recipe for leg of lamb roasted on a string over an open fire. We had invited a lot of people over, and since Andrew had wine tastings in the city, Mark and I worked all day in front of that fire, basting the lamb and cooking the potatoes and artichokes under the lamb drippings. When it was time to transport everything down to the house, and my back was breaking and my eyes were skinny slits from all of the smoke, Andrew poked his head around the gates, emerging from the dumpsters, giddy, half drunk and with black teeth from all of the wine and asked if he could help—just about eight hours too late.

It was a good dinner and everyone had fun. I was pretty tired and cleanup wasn't done until around 12:30 a.m. I still remember getting into bed that night aching from head to toe. Four hours later I went into labor with Elijah and he was born the following night at a birthing center in the city. We could only stay for twelve hours, so we slept there a couple of hours, and then packed up to take our tiny son home. On the way through Manhattan, Andrew was convinced that we needed to pick up some food to serve to people who were going to be coming to the house to meet Elijah, so we stopped into Ceci Cela for croissants and went by the restaurant for eggs and bacon. There was a constant trickle of visitors all day, and by nightfall, the house was packed. All of our friends were drinking pink Champagne and smoking cigars in the stairwell, and then at 11:30 p.m., everyone was hungry again. Caroline threw together pasta alla carbonara and we all sat and ate.

When Elijah was three, we acquired the lease to the pest management and supply store that was next door to the Diner. Andrew and I had visited a wine bar in Rome and another in Paris that we wanted to reincarnate. Mark had always dreamed of spending his days in a soccer bar, so we thought we'd marry the two concepts and were all excited planning and dreaming of our new spot. All of us, except Caroline, who was seriously pissed at Andrew for signing that lease. She was already working every day and unable to attract good cooks, so adding the responsibility of finding and managing another kitchen staff was too much to take.

When we first opened Marlow & Sons, it was the saddest place on the block. No one wanted to eat oysters and meats and cheeses for dinner, and there weren't enough soccer fans to keep the place full. People would come in, sit down, look at the menu, get up, and walk over to the Diner to eat. We realized that we had to make a decision between turning Marlow & Sons into a bar with no food, or turning it into a restaurant and building a kitchen downstairs. We went for the latter, and in hindsight, it feels like everything changed overnight.

Since I am writing the introduction, I will take this opportunity to take credit for as much as I can. That is part of the deal, right? I had been nagging Andrew about how great our waiter, Jason Schwartz, at the Diner was and kept asking him to promote him to management. Andrew likes to take things slower than I do, so he asked him to come over to Marlow to wait tables, even though it was Loserville over there. Jason believed in Marlow & Sons, and his intrinsic coolness convinced everyone else to believe in it, too. His music, his sense of humor, and his confidence in that place was exactly what Marlow needed. You can't start a fire without a spark, or a Schwartz, as it were.

Caroline finally got her prayers answered and kitchen talent started walking through the door. I remember the day in 2005 when Andrew and I were sitting outside at lunch and Sean Rembold jogged up to our table, squatted down in front of us, and accepted the job of sous chef. He was taking such a risk leaving his job working his way up the ranks at Bayard's down on Wall Street, but he was bursting with excitement. I can still remember the burn from the high five he gave us when he decided to come on board.

At Marlow we had been trying to run a wine bar menu featuring oysters, meats, and cheeses, which apparently wasn't what our customers wanted. Sean had a new and exciting take on what the food at Marlow & Sons could be: fried corn with shrimp butter, rabbit burgers, braised pork over grits with a bright salad on top. Sean's food was exciting: the electric mix of rich and meaty, buttery and fatty, bright and crunchy, and sweet all rolled together in one perfect bite.

Sean was soon joined in the kitchen by David Gould—a cocky twenty-three-year old—who memorably ordered a pint of beer at the bar while he waited for Caroline to interview him. It seems like an impossible thing to do, but Dave could do it. He knew, and still knows, that his tremendous talent could back up any kind of questionable behavior. Dave has the most delicate, magical hands, and each bite of his food is filled with so much delicious sexiness that you could take a bite and think that he was in love with you.

With Jason creating his special brand of front-of-house alchemy and Caroline, Sean, and Dave in the kitchens, our restaurants were exploding. People wanted to be there. Everyone was working hard and late and having fun. I can't really speak to the parties in those years, because Elijah and I were always home by 9 p.m., but I know that there was a lot of dancing on tables late into the night.

Diner and Marlow & Sons became magnets for exceptionally fun and talented people, and the best part is that the revolving staff of the first several years was a thing of the past. People who joined us during those years are still integrally a part of what we do and how we have expanded today. What would our life look like if Anna Dunn hadn't walked through our doors? She started by making coffee at Marlow & Sons and soon became one of the most important people in Andrew's life—a brother and a consigliere. We had started *Diner Journal* in 2006 with Caroline because we wanted to share her recipes and stories about our farmers, our life, and the things that we cared about, but with all of us overextended, it soon lost steam. Anna took the *Diner Journal* on in every way and poured her passion for words and art and food into each issue.

In 2011, Becky Johnson went to Marlow alone for her birthday one night and sat at the bar and ate a brick chicken and a piece of cheese for dessert. Even though she had promised herself that she wouldn't work in restaurants again, she was waiting tables for us a month later. She stayed under the radar until she started doing her telltale lettering on the Marlow & Sons menu board. Within a couple of months, she became the art director for the *Diner Journal.* Leah Campbell came to us straight from college as an intern for the *Diner Journal* and is now the communications director for all of our businesses. Julia Gillard lied about having bartending experience to get a job at the Diner. When Jason hired her, he said, "Listen, Merica said you are the best, so you're hired. She and I did psychedelics together back in the day down South. Do you know about wine?" With her unique point of view and eye for detail, Julia has become the photo editor for *Diner Journal* as well as a kind of artist-in-residence at the Diner.

As we continued to grow our staff, more and more people we admired wanted to participate. Ken Wiss ran the McCarren Park Greenmarket, where we spent every Saturday morning during the summer months. Who knew that he had been trying to get up the gumption to ask Caroline if he could work in the kitchen? As the story goes, he had decided that he would approach Caroline at the end of the summer in 2004, when she was doing a cooking demo, but as the moment approached for him to ask her if he could work in her kitchen, the conversation changed course, and he lost his nerve and decided he would wait until the following year to ask her. Good thing he finally did, because his delight with the flow of the seasons and the reverence for our farmers overflows from each bite of his food. There is no better moment in the spring than when Ken is cruising around our corner of the world, exclaiming for all to hear: "The ramps are here!" Whether he is making fried rice with lamb offal and house-fermented kimchi, or a sweet-and-sour pickled cayenne pepper and garlic scape relish, he makes you fall in love with each seasonal ingredient.

In 2008, twenty-three-year-old Scarlett Lindeman moved from Los Angeles to Brooklyn and started at Marlow & Sons under Caroline, Sean, and Dave. She was so young and sure of herself, funny, and good at everything. Everyone was attracted to her and wanted to be around her. When Dave moved over to start Roman's in 2009, he poached "Young Scarlett." Her spark lingers in everything she touches. Later she joined the *Diner Journal* team, and when Caroline left, she took over all of the cooking, recipe testing, editing, and writing.

Lee Desrosiers came to us in 2009 straight from working three jobs on Cape Cod. He had been making wine, working on a farm, and working with an oyster fisherman. He had no experience working in a kitchen, but wanted to cook and was desperate for a job. Sean took one look at the résumé and said to Lee, "So you know how to work and you can shuck oysters." He gave him a job working the oyster station at Marlow & Sons and making salads at the Diner. Lee is always the first to volunteer to help on every one of Andrew's doomed-from-the-start off-site cooking adventures, and he is always the one who turns the ill-fated event into a wild success.

With the restaurants now brimming with talent, we were inspired to open more and more businesses. We opened Roman's in Fort Greene in 2009 with Dave. We opened the Reynard and the Wythe Hotel in North Williamsburg in 2012 with Sean and Jason, and so that Ken could take over the chef position at both the Diner and Marlow & Sons. Anna is editor of *Diner Journal*, which is now in its ninth year. We started She Wolf Bakery with Austin Hall, who is the singular talent behind our bread, and Lee Desrosiers is now the chef of Achilles Heel, the riverside bar we opened in 2013.

The years keep passing, and sharing food with these people is at the core of what gives us meaning and what makes us happy. Our friends have started families of their own, moved away, embarked on their own projects, and missed a lamb dinner or two at our house. We've felt inspired to create this book—for them and for our beloved customers who have supported us since the time when we served mashed potatoes with every entrée at the Diner. Andrew and I have made each of these dinners every year for the people that we love the most, so we wanted to write them all down and give them to you, so that you can take them on your way and make them for the people that you love the most.

There is no getting around the fact that these dishes are challenging. They take days of thought, gathering, and psyching yourself up. Cassoulet. Paella. Tajine. Ragù. We chose to tackle them because these are all dishes we don't make in the restaurant kitchens. It is also in the effort of challenging ourselves, in risking total failure that we show our guests how very much we love and care about them. These meals are thrilling to make and share for the very same reason: the greater the risk, the greater the reward. So to all of you who have happened our way, we love you, and this book is our love song to you that we love so dearly and have chosen to spend our lives with. We hope that you find that cooking these meals together is as meaningful and rewarding as we do, and we hope that you remember our table and how much we are, and will always be, in your debt.

COLD NIGHT CASSOULET

DUCK LEG CONFIT

CASSOULET

CAMEMBERT *with* QUINCE CHUTNEY

DRUNKEN SAILOR CHOCOLATE CAKE

Dinner for 8 to 10

Cassoulet is named for its vessel, a large, pot with slanting sides made of earthenware or clay. Any oven-safe, heavy-bottomed ceramic or cast-iron pot that is at least 12 inches in diameter will stand in nicely. I've never asked Caroline why she chose to make cassoulet for Diner's opening night, but I can't imagine it any other way. Caroline and I were still practically strangers then, and as we walked the cassoulet up the hill in the snow, she told me where each ingredient came from. The duck legs for the confit were from Chinatown, and the bacon and sausage were from a butcher in Little Italy. The Tarbais beans were from Phipps Farm in Pescadero, California, a place Caroline liked to visit. This would be the first of countless conversations like it.

DUCK LEG CONFIT

Confit duck legs can be drawn from the snowcap of fat to use in cassoulets, stews, and salads and can be stored for several months in the refrigerator. Duck or goose fat will be readily available at your butcher shop.

6 duck legs

¼ cup kosher salt

Several sprigs thyme

Several sprigs rosemary

1 handful cracked peppercorns

4 cloves garlic, peeled and smashed

4 cups duck fat

Season the duck legs with the salt, sprigs of thyme, peppercorns, and garlic. Place in a shallow container and let cure covered overnight in the refrigerator.

The next day, preheat the oven to 225°F. In a saucepan, slowly warm the duck fat until it is liquid. Brush the cure off of the duck legs and place them in a pan that's small enough that the duck legs can fit snugly and will be completely submerged in the melted fat. Pour the fat over the duck legs and slide the pan into the oven. Bake until the duck legs are tender and the meat can easily be pulled from the bone, about 3 to 6 hours. Remove the pan from the oven and let the duck legs cool completely. Store covered in the refrigerator. The duck will be ready to use once the legs are completely chilled. Consider the duck preserved for days, weeks, months, or for the brave, perhaps a year.

CASSOULET

Like many of the dinners in these pages, cassoulet should be started a few days before you plan to share it with your friends. Finding enough time to prepare it will always be your biggest challenge. Keep in mind that cassoulet is a very rich dish, so smaller portions per person will do.

1½ pounds boneless pork shoulder

Kosher salt and freshly ground pepper

2 pounds dried Tarbais beans or cannellini beans

1 bunch sage

1 head garlic, halved lengthwise, unpeeled, plus 4 peeled cloves

⅓ cup duck fat

1 pound thick-cut bacon

1 (1½-pound) ham hock

4 confit duck legs (page 16)

2 medium onions, chopped

3 small carrots, diced

2 ribs celery, diced

1 tablespoon tomato paste

2 quarts unsalted chicken stock

2 sprigs parsley

1 small bunch thyme

2 bay leaves

1 (6-inch) square uncured pork skin

1 stale baguette

Olive oil

1 small bunch parsley, leaves chopped

3 leaves fresh sage, minced

3 sprigs oregano, leaves chopped

Two days before you plan to serve the cassoulet, season the pork shoulder with salt and pepper and soak the beans overnight in plenty of water. The next day, drain, rinse the beans, and put them in a large or medium pot with plenty of cold water, the sage, and the halved garlic. Bring to a bare simmer and cook for 1 hour. Cut the heat, add a handful of salt, and let the beans sit on the stove top while you proceed with the recipe.

Melt the duck fat in a pan over low heat and slowly brown the bacon on both sides until crisp. Transfer the bacon to a platter. Brown the ham hock on all sides in the duck fat and transfer to the platter with the bacon. Do the same with your pork shoulder. Slowly warm the confit duck legs in the fat and transfer to the platter. Let the legs cool slightly, then pick the meat and discard the skin and bones. Cut the pork shoulder into large cubes, with a good amount of fat left intact.

CONTINUED

In an earthenware or heavy-bottomed pot, add the onions, carrots, celery, and duck fat from your pan, season with salt and pepper, and sauté until soft and golden. Add the tomato paste, mashing it with a spoon. Add the chicken stock and bring to a simmer. With kitchen twine, tie the parsley, thyme, and bay leaves together and submerge the herbs in the stock. Roll and tie the pork skin with twine and add to the stock. Add the beans and simmer for an hour, then cut the heat. Submerge the ham hock, pulled duck meat, pork shoulder and bacon into the pot of beans. Cover and refrigerate overnight.

The day you'll serve the cassoulet, preheat the oven to 325°F. Remove the herbs and pork skin from the pot and discard. Retrieve the garlic head from the pot and squeeze the softened cloves out of their papery skins and stir into the cassoulet. On a cutting board, mash the 4 peeled garlic cloves to a paste with a pinch of salt—the slow-cooked garlic will be nice and sweet, while the fresh garlic provides punch—and stir the garlic paste into the cassoulet. Bring the cassoulet to a simmer, then slide it into the oven and bake for an hour.

Meanwhile, trim the crust from the baguette. Cut into cubes, spread out on a baking sheet, and bake until dry to the touch. Pulse the dried bread in a food processor until large crumbs form. Toss with olive oil and season with salt and pepper. Return to the baking sheet and bake until crisp and golden, about 10 minutes. Toss the bread crumbs with the parsley, sage, and oregano. Sprinkle the bread crumbs over the top of the cassoulet and bake for 30 minutes more. Remove from the oven and let the cassoulet sit on the counter for 10 minutes while you test your resolve.

CAMEMBERT *with* QUINCE CHUTNEY

Quince, rumored to be the forbidden fruit of the Garden of Eden, would prove a temptation so tough it actually could not be consumed. Quince needs to be cooked. Another perfect allegory for opening the doors of Diner; we had no idea what we were in for. However, to give you a sense of what you are in for, this recipe will make about 4 cups of chutney.

4 quince, peeled, quartered, and cored

½ cup of white wine

½ cup sugar

1 cinnamon stick

2 strips lemon peel

Pinch of kosher salt

¼ cup water

½ cup golden sultana raisins

½ cup Thompson raisins

1 (1-inch) knob ginger, peeled and minced

Freshly ground pepper

1 (8-ounce) wheel Camembert cheese or another soft tangy cheese, at room temperature

Sturdy walnut bread

Preheat the oven to 350°F. Place the quince in a roasting pan with the white wine, sugar, cinnamon stick, lemon peel, salt, and water. Stir to combine. Roast until the quince are just tender, about an hour. Let the quince cool completely, then dice. Transfer the diced quince to a small pot along with their roasting juices. Add the raisins and ginger and season with salt and pepper. Cook over low heat until the raisins are plumped. Let cool to room temperature, then adjust the seasoning. Remove and discard the cinnamon and lemon peel. Serve with the cheese and bread.

DRUNKEN SAILOR CHOCOLATE CAKE

This recipe comes from the *Stars Desserts* cookbook by Emily Luchetti, albeit slightly altered, because we always like to sneak in a bit more booze. Serve this cake late at night, with eight to ten spoons. No plates.

6 ounces bittersweet chocolate, chopped

10 tablespoons unsalted butter

¾ cup dark rum

4 eggs, separated

1¼ cups sugar

1 cup all-purpose flour

½ teaspoon kosher salt

8 ounces bittersweet chocolate, chopped

1 cup heavy cream

Preheat the oven to 350°F. Line a 9-inch cake pan with parchment paper. Melt the chocolate, butter, and rum in double boiler. Set aside and let cool slightly. In a bowl, whisk the egg yolks and ½ cup plus 3 tablespoons of the sugar until thickened, about 3 minutes. Stir in the melted chocolate mixture, then the flour and salt. Put the egg whites in the bowl of a stand mixer and whisk on medium speed until frothy, then continue whisking until soft peaks form. Add the remaining ½ cup plus 1 tablespoon sugar and continue whisking until stiff peaks form, about 5 minutes. Fold ⅓ of the egg whites into the chocolate batter, then fold in the remaining whites. Pour the batter into the prepared cake pan. Bake until a toothpick or cake tester inserted into the center of the cake comes out clean, 30 to 35 minutes. Let cool to room temperature.

In the meantime, make your glaze. Melt together the chocolate and heavy cream in a double boiler. Set aside and let cool to room temperature. When your cake is cool, unmold it, place on a cake stand, and remove the parchment paper. Frost the cake with the glaze. Hold on to the spoons for an hour before releasing the hounds.

RAGÙ AT THE END OF WINTER

FRIDAY NIGHT AT THE BUTCHER SHOP

SATURDAY MORNING

AFTER LUNCH

SUNDAY, AROUND NOON

THE CODA & THE COPPA

VINEGAR & PEPPERS

FRUIT & BISCOTTI

Sunday sauce for 8 to 10

Think of this ragù as the Sunday matinee. Serve it in the afternoon, when you can still glimpse low angular light arching through the window. Dave Gould, the chef of Roman's, taught me to eat this ragù in three acts, with pasta as the first course, braised meats the second, and salad the third. It could be four courses if you considered biscotti and Vin Santo to finish.

Serious, contemplative, slow. The ragù is culturally distinct, harking back to a time and place where meat needed to be stewed. There is a satisfying economy in making two dishes in one. Braising meat in the tomatoes not only transforms the rougher cuts, but it also enriches the sauce for the pasta.

Preparing this ragù will take a weekend. After the holidays and the celebration of a new year, consider the making of this sauce as a welcome distraction, a practice, to carry you through the long winter months and short winter days.

FRIDAY NIGHT AT THE BUTCHER SHOP

Make a list. Lose the list. Make another. Coppa can be hard to find; ask your local butcher. If it's unavailable, pork shoulder or butt or anything that braises well will work. Also ask your butcher to grind your prosciutto and pancetta. If she is too busy you can alternatively finely chop or pulse in a food processor.

1 rack meaty pork ribs, broken down into manageable pieces

2 pounds pork coppa, tied into a roast

3 pounds veal shanks

1 pound oxtail, cut into 1-inch pieces

Olive oil, for browning and for drizzling

1 onion, chopped

2 small carrots, chopped

2 ribs celery, chopped

1 sweet pepper, seeded and chopped

1 small bunch basil

2 cups red wine

¾ cup tomato paste

5 (28-ounce) cans crushed tomatoes

½ pound ground beef

½ pound ground pork

2 ounces finely ground prosciutto

2 ounces finely ground pancetta

2 eggs

½ cup grated Pecorino Romano

½ cup grated Parmigiano-Reggiano

2 cups crustless bread cubes

1 cup ragù sauce (page 32)

Salt and freshly ground pepper

Olive oil, for frying

1 pound mild pork sausage

Heavily season the pork ribs, coppa, veal shanks, and oxtail with salt and refrigerate overnight.

SATURDAY MORNING

Once the coffee has been made, pull out your seasoned pork ribs, coppa, veal shanks, and oxtail from the refrigerator, set on the counter, and let come to room temperature. It's a bit of work to practice restraint when you're cooking all Saturday for dinner on Sunday. You'll get hungry, so plan a lunch for yourself while you are meditating on (and with) the sauce. Salami on toast, with chunks of Pecorino on the side, and a salad of greens. Whatever is easy.

Working in batches, gently brown the pork ribs, coppa, veal shanks, and oxtail in oil over medium-low heat in a large Dutch oven. Be careful to prevent the oil from smoking or overcrowding the pot. Take the time to brown every surface of the meats, transferring the browned pieces to a platter while the other cuts have their turn. It will take almost an hour. If the smoke alarm goes off, the pot is probably too hot. If the smoke alarm doesn't go off, you probably haven't done your job. Once all of the meats are browned, pour off most of the rendered fat and discard. Start your sauce by adding the onion, carrots, celery, sweet pepper, and basil to the pot and cook over medium heat until softened. Add the red wine and boil off the alcohol for a minute or two. Add tomato paste and stir until dissolved. Add crushed tomatoes and bring to a simmer. Return the browned meats to the pot, bring the sauce back to a boil, then lower the heat to the gentlest simmer possible.

Cover the pot and let simmer, adding a splash of water from time to time. Herein lies the balancing act. Over the next several hours you want the flavors of the sauce to concentrate and then open up. When the ragù starts to resemble the consistency of porridge, add a little water and then let it reduce again. You'll want to reduce the ragù several times, coaxing more flavor each time. Wander away from the stove but stay vigilant. Continue to cook until the meat is uniformly tender but not completely falling apart, around 3 to 4 hours.

AFTER LUNCH

To make the meatballs, mix the beef, pork, prosciutto, pancetta, eggs, and cheeses in a large bowl. In another bowl, soak the bread cubes in a cup of the ragù sauce. With your hands, work the bread and sauce into a paste, then fold it into the meat and cheese mixture. Season with salt and pepper and form into small meatballs. It's fine if they are a bit misshapen; the sauce forgives.

Heat the oil in a sauté pan over medium heat and panfry the meatballs until just cooked through, turning to get a good crust on all of the sides, about 20 minutes. Transfer the meatballs to a baking sheet lined with a kitchen towel to drain.

Lower the heat slightly and gently brown the sausage in the same pan until just cooked through, about 15 minutes. Sink the sausages and meatballs into the ragù and make sure that everything is covered by the sauce. By now the ragù has been braising for almost 4 hours.

Turn off the heat and let the ragù come to room temperature and sit for at least 2 hours. Cover and refrigerate overnight, which will let excess fat rise to the surface.

SUNDAY, AROUND NOON

The shape of pasta should be carefully considered and debated.

2 pounds maccheroni, or maybe penne, cavatelli, or rigatoni

Enough ragù to sauce the pasta (page 32)

Grated Parmigiano-Reggiano

Preheat the oven to 300°F. Pull the ragù from the refrigerator. While it's still cold, skim the fat off the top and discard. Transfer the meat from the ragù to an oven-safe vessel and spoon a good layer of sauce over the top. Cover and warm in the oven while you get the pasta going. Warm the remaining sauce over medium heat on the stove.

Cook the pasta in salted water until it is a few minutes shy of al dente, then transfer the pasta to the pot with the reserved sauce. Cook the pasta gently for its last few minutes, just until al dente, so the pasta can soak up some of the complexity of the ragù. For a first course, serve a small portion of the pasta and sprinkle it with a little Parmigiano-Reggiano. Restraint is romantic.

THE CODA & THE COPPA

Country bread, for serving

When the pasta course has been cleared away, pull the pot of braising meats from the oven. Slice the coppa and the ribs into manageable portions. Make sure that all of the meat is warm throughout, then arrange a platter of sliced veal shanks, coppa, ribs, meatballs, sausages, and oxtail. Spoon the leftover sauce from the pot on the stove over the meats and drizzle with a little olive oil. Serve with crusty bread.

VINEGAR & PEPPERS

The brightness, acidity, and crunch of these sweet peppers hold up well to the richness of the ragù. They also provide a pleasing accent of color. If you can't readily find the peppers listed below at a local farm or market, any thin-skinned sweet pepper will do.

1 pound firm, thin-skinned sweet peppers, such ascubanelle, sigaretta di Bergamo, or sweet habanero, seeded and cut into bite-size rounds

Olive oil

½ cup red wine vinegar

1 tablespoon sugar

Kosher salt

Small pinch of dried oregano

½ cup thinly sliced carrot

½ cup thinly sliced red onion

½ cup pitted Gaeta or Kalamata olives

1 pound mixed chicories, such as radicchio, escarole, frisée, or Treviso, torn into large pieces

½ cup fresh parsley, chopped

½ lemon

Working in batches, sear the peppers in a little olive oil in a small pan. The peppers should take on a bit of color but still maintain their crunch. Deglaze the pan with the vinegar, then pour the peppers and vinegar into a high-sided bowl. Stir in the sugar and a large pinch of salt until they dissolve. When the peppers are just slightly cooled, fold in the oregano, carrot, onion, and olives. Let marinate at room temperature for at least 20 minutes or overnight covered in the refrigerator.

When ready to serve, toss the chicories with the pepper mixture. Add the parsley, a squeeze of lemon, and season with salt, if needed. Finish with a little good olive oil.

FRUIT & BISCOTTI

There's something about a small glass of Vin Santo on the table in front of you, with a plum in one hand and a cookie in the other. Dip your cookie in the sweet wine for just a note of sweetness. It will ease you out of the late afternoon, and into the night.

4 cups all-purpose flour

1 cup sugar

1 teaspoon baking powder

1 teaspoon kosher salt

3 eggs

⅓ cup olive oil, plus more for brushing

Zest of 1 lemon

1 cup almonds, toasted and chopped

1 tablespoon fennel seeds

Damson or cherry plums or pears

Preheat the oven to 350°F. Sift together the flour, sugar, baking powder, and salt. In a large bowl, whisk together the eggs, olive oil, and lemon zest. Add the flour mixture and stir to create dough. With your hands, knead in the almonds and fennel seeds. The dough will be pretty dry at first. This will take a little patience and elbow grease but fear not. It will all come together. Turn the dough onto a lightly floured counter, divide in half, and form into balls. Roll the balls out from the center into two logs, about three inches wide, as if you were making a clay snake in arts and crafts.

Flatten the logs and place on an oiled baking sheet. Bake for 30 to 40 minutes. Pull the baking sheet from the oven and lower the heat to 275°F. Transfer the logs to a cutting board while they are still warm. Use a serrated knife to cut the biscotti into slices on the diagonal, that are about ½ inch thick. Return the biscotti, faceup, to the baking sheet. Bake for 15 to 20 minutes more, until dry and lightly golden. Pull from the oven and brush each biscotti with a little olive oil. Allow to cool and serve with booze and the fruit. Biscotti can be stored for 3 weeks.

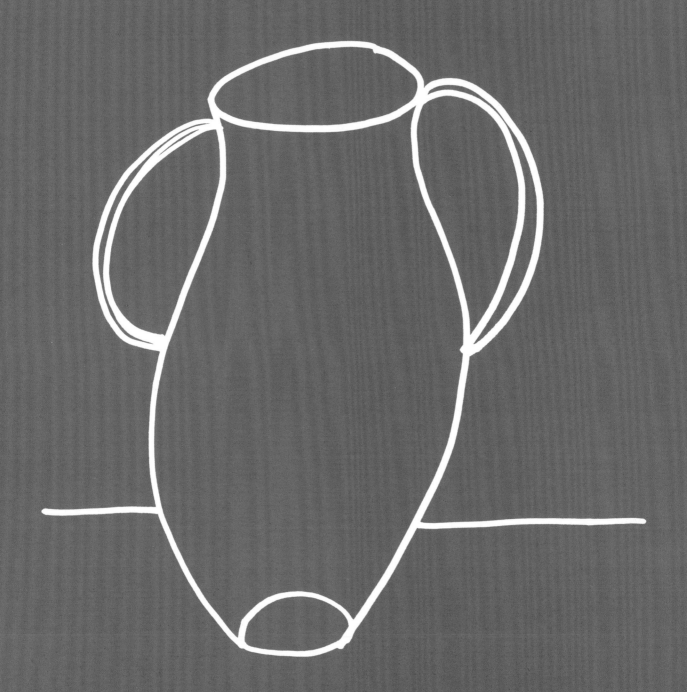

LULU'S
LEG OF LAMB

ROASTED LEG OF LAMB & POTATOES DRESSED DOWN *with* ZEST

HARISSA

BREAD SALSA

SNAP PEAS COOKED IN BUTTER

WHEN IT COMES TO BABY ARTICHOKES

YELLOW TART

Birthday dinner for 15

Preparing a leg of lamb feels like a symbolic act, an offering. The first time Kate made this, she cooked the lamb in the stone fireplace behind Diner. She hung it on a string over embers, where it cooked, spinning, touched by rosemary. She was conjuring Lulu Peyraud and willing our first son, Elijah, to be born.

We never planned to throw a large party at our house to welcome our first child into our lives, but after he was born, we decided it would be a tradition for all the future babes we hoped to have. We saw what an important role our friends would have in our kids' lives, and so every year on Elijah's birthday, we cook lamb, and snap peas, get the mortar and pestle out, and make bread salsa and harissa. Just as every year on Béa's birthday, we gather together to make paella. It's become a yearly tradition in honor of each kid, to prepare a meal symbolic of their day of birth.

ROASTED LEG OF LAMB & POTATOES DRESSED DOWN *with* ZEST

If you can roast this lamb on a string over an open flame, then make sure you leave the bone in. For conventional ovens, ask your butcher for two legs of lamb, de-boned. You'll want all the potatoes to be about the same size. Medium to large fingerling potatoes are perfect for this roast.

2 boneless legs of lamb

Kosher salt and freshly ground pepper

12 anchovy fillets

12 cloves garlic, peeled

¼ cup rosemary, minced

5 pounds fingerling potatoes, scrubbed and unpeeled

1 lemon

Season the lamb legs inside and out with salt and pepper. With a large mortar and pestle, pound the anchovies, garlic, and rosemary into a paste. Rub the paste all over the lamb, really massaging it in. Roll up the lamb and secure it with kitchen twine; finally, a chance to practice your knot-tying skills. Cover and refrigerate overnight.

Two hours before dinner, remove the lamb legs from the refrigerator. Preheat the oven to 425°F. Place the potatoes in the bottom of a large roasting pan. Pour the olive oil over the potatoes and season well with salt and pepper. Place the lamb legs on top of the potatoes. Roast for 20 minutes, then lower the heat to 350°F. Continue to roast until the internal temperature is 135°F, 45 to 60 minutes. Remove from the oven, transfer to a platter and let rest for 30 minutes.

After the lamb has rested, pour any juices that have collected on the platter into the roasting pan with the potatoes. Toss to coat the potatoes in the juices, then taste one. If they need more salt, add some now. If they seem dry, add oil and toss to coat. Zest the lemon over the potatoes, then cut the lemon in half and squeeze one half over the potatoes. Toss the potatoes until they are well dressed. Carve the roast into thin slices and serve with the potatoes on the side.

HARISSA

Harissa is a piquant condiment from Tunisia. Our friend and the former sous chef of Diner, Ben Jackson, started serving it with eggs and fish. Soon enough we wanted it on everything. You can never have enough condiments. Harissa brings a nice spice to the lamb. This recipe yields about 2 cups.

- 1 tablespoon cumin seeds
- 1 tablespoon coriander seeds
- 1 tablespoon caraway seeds
- 1 teaspoon peppercorns
- 6 cloves garlic, peeled and smashed
- 1 cup olive oil
- 4 dried chiles de árbol, stemmed
- 6 roasted piquillo peppers or any sweet roasted red pepper and some of their liquor
- 2 tablespoons sweet smoked paprika
- 1 tablespoon brown sugar
- Kosher salt

In a dry skillet over medium heat, toast the cumin, coriander, caraway, and peppercorns until fragrant. Pour the spices into a bowl to cool. With a mortar and pestle, pound the spices into a powder. Toast the garlic in the olive oil in a small saucepan, swirling constantly, until the cloves are just golden. Do not let the garlic burn. Cut the heat and let the garlic sit in the oil while you rehydrate the chiles.

Pour boiling water over the chiles and let sit until rehydrated, about 30 minutes. Remove the garlic from the pan, reserving the oil. With a large mortar and pestle, pound the chiles, garlic, and piquillo peppers into a rough puree. Add the pounded spices, along with the paprika, sugar, and a splash of the pepper liquor, and stir until combined. Slowly incorporate the garlic oil, stirring rapidly with the pestle until the harissa is smooth. Season well with salt.

BREAD SALSA

Think of this as a vinaigrette that's made with bread. It's addicting and we think we may have stolen it from Alice Waters, from whom many great ideas have been lifted. Inspired? Ideas are free. This recipe will make approximately 2 cups.

3 cloves garlic

8 anchovy fillets

Leaves from 3 bunches parsley,
finely chopped

Leaves 1 small bunch oregano,
finely chopped

Leaves from 1 small bunch
summer savory, finely chopped

¼ cup capers, rinsed and chopped,
soaked in water if they are packed in salt

Kosher salt and freshly ground pepper

1 baguette

1 cup olive oil, for frying

Juice of 1 lemon

1 shallot, minced and macerated
in a splash of red wine vinegar

With a mortar and pestle, pound the garlic and then the anchovies into a paste. Stir together the mashed garlic and anchovies with the parsley, oregano, savory, capers, and enough olive oil to make a nice, wet salsa. Taste and season with salt and pepper. Set aside.

Trim the crust off the baguette and dice the bread. Pulse the bread in a food processor until large crumbs form. Set a sieve or fine colander over a heatproof bowl next to the stove. In a frying pan, working in batches, fry the bread crumbs in an inch or so of olive oil until golden brown. Stir constantly; the crumbs will color quickly. Pour the oil and bread crumbs into the sieve. Drain well and transfer the crumbs to a plate. Carefully return the hot oil to the pan and proceed with the remaining bread. Just before serving, whisk the lemon juice and macerated shallot and its liquid into the salsa. Stir in the bread crumbs. Serve with lamb or other roasted meats.

SNAP PEAS
COOKED IN BUTTER

A gentle pod, the snap pea is the opposite of the spiny artichoke. I'd eat them just for the color.

- 2 pounds snap peas
- Olive oil
- 1 shallot, minced
- Kosher salt and freshly ground pepper
- 8 tablespoons salted butter, cubed
- Leaves from 1 bunch mint
- Juice of 1 lemon
- A few scallions, sliced (optional)

Trim the snap peas of any sturdy stems. Get a large sauté pan going over high heat, add enough oil to coat, and let it get hot. Throw the snap peas and shallot in the pan. Toss and season with salt and pepper. Lower the heat and add the butter and a splash of water. Cook the snap peas, stirring occasionally, until they turn bright green and the butter melts, just a minute or two. Transfer to a bowl and toss with the mint and lemon juice. Eat a pea. Add more salt if necessary. Serve immediately.

WHEN IT COMES TO BABY ARTICHOKES

The thing about artichokes is that there are many different types. Sturdy, spiny, delicate, some baby, some giant. How to proceed, like writer David Tanis says, lies at the heart of the artichoke. Some baby artichokes need very little attention—their chokes are so soft that they can be eaten whole after removing a couple of the stiff outer leaves. Others may be small but still quite thorny and need to be fully trimmed. Artichokes are like oysters; it's amazing that we figured out how to eat them.

2 lemons

6 pounds baby artichokes

2 Meyer lemons, thinly sliced

Olive oil

Kosher salt

A splash of white wine

Leaves from 1 small bunch parsley

Get everything ready like a ninja, including a sharp, sturdy paring knife, or two, if you have friend. Processing an artichoke, like processing life, is always better with a friend. Get a big bowl of water. Cut the lemons in half and squeeze their juice into the water. Toss the spent lemon halves in, too. Place another bowl nearby for the artichoke scraps. Put Morrissey on the stereo. Preheat the oven to 375°F.

All artichokes, large and small, need a little trimming. Strip off a couple of the outside leaves, anything that's tough, brown, or old looking. Lop off its tip. Slice the artichoke lengthwise down the middle and inspect the choke. If it's tough and woody, you'll have to remove it, by scooping it out of the center. If it's tender, you can leave it the way it is. You want to leave as much of the artichoke as you can. There's not that much meat for the amount of work, so be prudent in your paring. Drop the trimmed artichokes into the bowl of water as you go.

Roast the Meyer lemon slices, dry, on a baking sheet until shrunken and chewy, 5 to 10 minutes. Set the slices aside to cool. Pull the artichokes from their bath and drain. Toss the artichokes with oil and lots of salt. Roast on another baking sheet until they can be pierced with a knife, about 15 minutes. If you like, you can roast them a little longer, 5 minutes or so, until golden. Pull the baking sheet and splash with the white wine to deglaze. Transfer the artichokes and any residual juice to a bowl and combine with the roasted Meyer lemon slices and parsley.

YELLOW TART

Lemon custard tart feels a little like eating sunshine when you're longing for the summer, conceptual sunshine. Neale Holaday, the pastry chef at Marlow & Sons and Diner, wrote this recipe for us.

16 tablespoons unsalted butter, at room temperature

½ cup sugar

1 egg

2¾ cups all-purpose flour

¼ teaspoon baking powder

¼ teaspoon kosher salt

1 sheet silver-strength gelatin

12 egg yolks

2 cups sugar

1 scant cup freshly squeezed lemon juice

1 tablespoon lemon zest

½ teaspoon kosher salt

18 tablespoons unsalted butter, cubed

Silver-strength gelatin acts just like powdered gelatin but dissolves more evenly. If you can't find it sheeted, powdered is fine. A tablespoon powdered gelatin will equal 3 sheets gelatin.

Preheat the oven to 325°F. To make the tart shell, cream the butter and sugar together in a bowl with an electric mixer until light and fluffy, about 5 minutes. Add the egg and beat until fully combined. Fold in the flour, baking powder, and salt until a dough forms. Turn the dough out onto the counter and form into a ball. Roll the dough between 2 pieces of parchment paper until it's about ¼ inch thick. Transfer the dough to a 9-inch tart shell. Trim any overhang with a sharp knife and prick the bottom with a fork. Bake until golden brown, 10 to 15 minutes. Let cool while you make the custard.

To make the custard, soak the gelatin in cold water for 5 to 10 minutes to bloom. Prepare an ice bath by filling a large bowl with ice and cold water and set aside. In another bowl, whisk together the egg yolks, sugar, lemon juice, lemon zest, and salt. Transfer the egg yolk mixture to a pot and cook over low heat, whisking constantly, until the mixture thickens and coats the back of a spoon, 3 to 5 minutes. Cut the heat immediately. Wring the gelatin of any excess water and whisk it into the egg yolk mixture along with the butter until the gelatin dissolves and the butter melts. Strain the custard through a fine-mesh sieve into a bowl and set the bowl in the ice bath. Stir constantly until the custard cools, then pour into the prepared tart shell. Refrigerate overnight or for at least 1 hour before serving.

AGRO & DOLCE

BEETS ROASTED UNTIL THE END OF TIME

HOMEMADE YOGURT

WHY A WHEY SMOOTHIE

OLIVE & ROSEMARY FOCACCIA

SAFFRON ARTICHOKES

SARDINES EN SAOR

COD with POLENTA, TOMATO, & MINT

Lunch for 8

Agrodolce is a metaphor for life. You have to have balance. It is, perhaps, what all things reduce to. This menu is classic Dave Gould. Dave is always agro, and he is always dolce. As a chef, he has to approach every day with real gusto, which can be thought of as agro, as well as real sweetness, so he can coax flavors and cooks to do their best.

Our wine director Lee Campbell chose René and Agnès Mosse's Moussamoussettes—a lively, pink, bubbly, and unfiltered wine—to accompany Dave's menu. René Mosse has long been one of our favorite winemakers. He, like Dave, is a sweet-and-sour pirate.

BEETS ROASTED
UNTIL THE END OF TIME

Too bad there's no thyme in the recipe. Feel free to add herbs at will.

8 large beets

Olive oil

Kosher salt

1 teaspoon red pepper flakes

1 teaspoon fennel seeds

1 teaspoon dried oregano

2 tablespoons red wine vinegar

1½ cups yogurt (page 62)

2 ripe, juicy oranges, peeled with
a knife and cut into slices

Handful of torn dates, pits removed

½ cup raw pistachios, chopped
(look for the good Sicilian kind)

Coarse sea salt

Preheat the oven to 350°F. Peel the beets and cut into large wedges. Toss the beets with the oil, salt, red pepper flakes, fennel seeds, oregano, and a splash of vinegar. Spread out the beets on a baking sheet and roast, stirring frequently, until softened, shriveled, and jammy, 1½ to 2 hours. Be sure to stir the beets even more frequently during the last 30 minutes so they don't burn. Let the beets cool slightly, then toss with a bit more oil and a touch more vinegar. Let marinate for at least 30 minutes.

When ready to serve, arrange dollops of yogurt on a platter, then spoon the beets and their juices all around. Arrange the oranges over the beets and scatter the dates and pistachios on top. Drizzle with olive oil and any accumulated orange juice left on your cutting board, and sprinkle coarse sea salt on top.

HOMEMADE YOGURT

I feel conflicted about telling you to buy yogurt to make yogurt. It feels redundant, or like when you defined a word in elementary school using that word. You can just buy yogurt, or you can follow this recipe and never need to buy yogurt again. This will make more than what you need for the beet recipe, but it can be used to start future batches of yogurt. Cultivate the culture of your own house.

2 quarts whole milk

2 tablespoons unflavored good-quality whole milk yogurt

In a pot over medium heat, bring the milk to 180°F, just below a simmer, stirring frequently. Cut the heat and let the milk sit until the temperature drops to 115°F. Whisk in the yogurt. Transfer the mixture to a plastic or ceramic container, and let sit in a warm spot overnight, 10 to 24 hours, until the milk thickens into yogurt. Strain the yogurt through a cheesecloth set over a large bowl. Reserve the whey for smoothies or braises. Don't throw it down the sink; use everything. Refrigerate the yogurt until ready to use.

WHY A WHEY SMOOTHIE

We make this in the morning when we are not awake enough to measure. Here is an approximation. Adjust to your liking.

1 cup reserved whey from homemade yogurt

1 egg

¼ teaspoon vanilla extract

2 tablespoons raw cocoa powder

1 tablespoon honey

Large handful of ice

Blend all the ingredients until smooth. Drink quickly. Breakfast of champions.

OLIVE & ROSEMARY FOCACCIA

This recipe comes from Austin Hall, the head baker of She Wolf Bakery. We started She Wolf late at night in the Roman's kitchen in 2009. Dave had been wanting to develop a sourdough bread to accompany his menus. In the beginning, as Dave would be getting ready to leave at the end of a night's busy service, he'd build a hot fire in the wood oven and spread the coals across the deck. Austin would come in at 3 a.m., rake the coals, and let the oven come down to temp while he shaped his bread. Soon enough Austin was making bread for all of our restaurants, as well as to sell at the Greenmarket. This recipe is technical and thorough, just like the man himself. For the curious, the detail oriented, and the inspired.

Poolish, or mother dough, is a pre-ferment and is the bubbling cauldron at the center of any wild yeast dough. This is your starter. Make your poolish the day before serving, as it can take anywhere between 5 and 10 hours to develop. And buy a scale so you can follow the gram measurements. Baking is a science, a meditation on precision. This recipe will make two 10-inch rounds of focaccia.

2 scant cups (300 grams) all-purpose flour

1¼ cups (293 grams) lukewarm water (70°F)

Pinch of active dry yeast

1½ cups (225 grams) all-purpose flour

⅓ cup (50 grams) coarsely ground whole-grain flour
(such as wheat, spelt, or rye)

½ cup (118 grams) lukewarm water
(80°F if mixing by hand, or 70°F if using a stand mixer)

All of the poolish

1 scant teaspoon (3 grams) active dry yeast

5 teaspoons (12 grams) kosher salt

Olive oil

1 cup green olives, pitted and torn into pieces

Leaves from 3 sprigs rosemary, coarsely chopped

Sea salt

CONTINUED

To make your poolish, stir together the flour, water, and yeast in a large bowl. Cover and let sit and ferment at room temperature. Fermentation will happen faster in warmer temperatures and slower in cooler temperatures; 70°F is ideal. It can take up anywhere between 5 and 10 hours. When the poolish is ready to use, it will be loose and bubbly, with a nutty aroma. If you are in doubt, drop a pinch of the poolish into room temperature water. If it floats, it's good to go. If the poolish sinks, it needs more time to develop.

To make the focaccia, mix together the flours, water, and poolish in a large bowl with a wooden spoon until no dry bits of flour remain. Cover and let rest for about 30 minutes. As the dough rests, the flour absorbs the water and gluten begins to develop, even though the dough is not being kneaded. After 30 minutes, add the yeast and salt and mix, 8 to 10 minutes by hand with a wooden spoon or 2 to 3 minutes at high speed with an electric mixer. Turn out the dough into a lightly oiled bowl. Cover with a kitchen towel and let rest in a warm area (about 80°F) for 30 minutes.

Turn the dough out onto a lightly floured surface. With floured hands, gently give the bottom edge of the dough a little stretch and fold it toward the center of the dough, taking care not to tear it. Do the same for the top, left, and right sides. Gently grab the tidy little dough ball, flip it over, and drop it back into the oiled bowl. Cover and let rest for 30 minutes, then fold the dough a second time. Cover and let the dough rest for 30 minutes more. The dough should be about double its original size.

If you are unsure if the dough is ready to be shaped, dust your hands with flour and give the dough a gentle poke with your finger. If the indentation remains or closes up very slowly, the dough is ready. If the dough bounces back without holding the indentation, give it more time.

Generously oil two 9-inch round cake pans. To shape the focaccia, turn the dough out onto a floured surface and divide it in half. Gently form each piece into a ball and coat with oil. Place into the prepared cake pans and douse with more oil, probably more than you think you need, about 3 tablespoons. This will give the focaccia a good layer of oil to fry in.

Place a pizza stone in the oven and preheat the oven to 450°F. Gently stretch each dough ball until it fills the cake pan and press indentations into it with your fingertips. Press half of the olives and rosemary down deeply into each dough, which will help keep them from getting forced to the surface during baking. Drizzle a little more olive oil into the indentations in the dough. Scatter the remaining olives and rosemary over the top of each focaccia and sprinkle with sea salt. Bake the focaccia until the top and sides just begin to brown, about 20 minutes.

SAFFRON ARTICHOKES

Braising is great way to handle the spiny heart of this vegetable.

2½ lemons

5 pounds large artichokes

4 cloves garlic,
peeled and smashed

Olive oil

¼ cup chopped fresh parsley

Large pinch of dried mint

Small pinch of dried oregano

Small pinch of saffron

2 leeks, white and light green parts,
halved, cleaned, and thinly sliced

1 carrot, peeled and thinly sliced

2 ribs celery, thinly sliced

2 plum tomatoes, fresh or canned,
crushed to a pulp with your hands

¼ cup dried porcini

Kosher salt

1 cup white wine

Get a big bowl of water. Cut 2 of the lemons in half and squeeze their juice into the water. Toss the spent lemon halves in, too. Place another bowl nearby for the artichoke scraps. Strip off a couple of the outside leaves, anything that's tough, brown, or old looking. Trim the tips. Slice the artichoke lengthwise into quarters or halves, depending on their size, and inspect the choke. If it's tough and woody, you'll have to scoop it out and discard. If it's tender, you can leave it the way it is. Drop the trimmed artichokes into the bowl of water as you go.

In a shallow pot, large enough to fit all artichokes in a single layer, gently cook the garlic in a healthy pour of olive oil, until light gold. Add the parsley, mint, oregano, and saffron and let them sizzle and infuse the oil for a minute or so. Add the leeks, carrots, celery, tomatoes, and porcini, season well with salt, stirring to combine, and gently cook until they soften but don't take on any color, about 15 minutes. Add the wine, raise the heat, and cook until the smell of alcohol dissipates.

Add the artichokes to the pot in a single layer, lower the heat, and gently simmer until they can be easily pierced with a paring knife, about 20 minutes. The cooking liquid should almost be high enough to submerge the artichokes, but not quite, so add a bit of water to the pan if it needs it.

It's important to be gentle with the artichokes as they cook; stir with a nimble hand. The artichokes should be juicy when finished. Once the artichokes are cooked, add salt to taste, gently folding it in; artichokes can absorb a considerable amount of salt, like beans. Let the mixture cool to room temperature before serving. Douse with olive oil and squeeze the remaining ½ lemon over the top.

SARDINES EN SAOR
OR WHAT TO DO WITH A LEFTOVER FISH

I like this recipe just for the alliteration alone. You could easily plan on fried sardines for dinner one night and then vinegar ones for lunch a few days later. Buy at least 2 sardines per person, or if you are planning on eating this for two meals, double down on the little fishes. So many sardines, so little time.

20 whole fresh sardines, scaled	½ cup sugar
2 cups all-purpose flour	Kosher salt
Neutral oil (such as grapeseed oil)	6 eggs
3 red onions, thinly sliced	Juice of 1 lemon
½ cup olive oil, plus more for finishing	Coarse salt
¾ cup raisins	Freshly cracked pepper
2 cups white wine vinegar	1 (4-inch) piece horseradish, peeled

Dredge the sardines in the flour, shaking off any excess. In a sturdy, shallow pot heat 2 inches of the neutral oil until it's 400°F. Working in batches, deep-fry the sardines until they're a deep golden brown. Flip the sardines and brown on the second side. The goal is to dehydrate the sardines and get them nice and brown, so fry long and slow, about 2 to 3 minutes on each side. Pull the sardines from the oil with tongs. Drain the fish on paper towels and let cool to room temperature.

In a sauté pan over medium heat, sauté the onions in the olive oil until they are translucent but still maintain some tooth, about 5 minutes. Add the raisins, vinegar, sugar, and 2 pinches of salt. Bring to a boil, then cut the heat. Place the sardines in a single layer in a shallow container. Pour the vinegar mixture over the sardines and drizzle with a little olive oil. Cover and refrigerate for at least 24 hours or up to 3 days.

On the day you are going to serve the sardines, prepare an ice bath. Bring a pot of water to a boil, then slip in the eggs for 7½ minutes. Transfer the eggs to the ice bath. When cool enough to touch, crack the shells and return them to the ice bath, submerging them until cooled, about 10 minutes or so.

When ready to serve, peel the eggs and quarter them. Arrange the sardines with the onions and all their juices on a platter. Top with the quartered eggs, drizzle with the lemon juice and oil, and sprinkle with coarse salt and cracked pepper. Grate lots of horseradish over the top. Serve chilled, between fridge and room temperature, like a chilly afternoon in Venice.

COD *with* POLENTA, TOMATO, & MINT

Though some cod populations have been seriously depleted, there are healthy fisheries in the Pacific, and Georges Bank in the Atlantic, as well as sustainable farms that are robust and well managed. If you are unsure, check the Monterey Bay Aquarium Seafood Watch app—it's the only app I love.

4 skinless cod fillets

Kosher salt

1½ teaspoons ground chile de árbol

Zest of 1 lemon

2 cups all-purpose flour

3 cloves garlic, peeled and sliced

2 tablespoons capers, soaked in water if salt packed

8 anchovy fillets

1 yellow onion, diced small

¾ cup pitted green olives (such as Lucques), with ⅓ cup brine

2 (28-ounce) cans whole tomatoes

Leaves from 1 small bunch mint

2 cups good-quality, coarse-grained polenta

8 cups water

2 tablespoons olive oil

Kosher salt

8 tablespoons unsalted butter, cubed

Freshly ground pepper

A day before you cook the cod, lightly season the fillets with salt and sprinkle with the chile and lemon zest. Refrigerate, uncovered, overnight.

To make the polenta, combine the polenta and water in a pot. Add the oil, season with salt, and cook over high heat, whisking constantly, until the polenta has thickened and is no longer falling to the bottom of the pot, about 5 minutes. Turn the heat as low as it will go and

CONTINUED

continue to gently cook the polenta, stirring often to make sure it isn't scorching the bottom of the pot. It's a thin margin between toasted and scorched. Keep your nose attuned; if it starts to smell at all burnt, you've gone too far.

When the polenta's texture is soft and creamy without any grittiness, cut the heat. The cooking time varies immensely among types of polenta, but it will probably take around 2 hours. Fold in the butter and season with salt and pepper. The polenta will hold, refrigerated, for up to 1 week. To reheat, gently warm in a pot over low heat.

To make the cod, pull it from the refrigerator and dredge it in the flour, shaking off any excess. Heat the oil in a sauté pan over medium heat and panfry the cod until both sides are golden, in batches, about 3 minutes per side. The fish may be slightly underdone at the center. Drain on paper towels.

In a shallow pot large enough to fit the cod in a single layer, heat a healthy pour of oil with the garlic, until the cloves start to take on a little color. Add the capers and fry for a minute or so. Add the anchovies, onion, and olives, stirring to combine, and sweat them until the onions soften, about 10 minutes. Add the olive brine and the tomatoes, stirring to combine. Bring to a boil, then lower the heat to a simmer. Taste and season with more salt and pepper if needed. Gently press the cod pieces into the sauce and cook until the cod is warm in the center, 5 to 10 minutes. Let the cod rest and cool to room temperature before serving. The cod will hold, refrigerated, for a couple of days. To reheat, warm gently on the stove top before serving.

When ready to serve, spoon the polenta onto a platter and arrange the cod and some of the tomato sauce over the polenta. Drizzle with olive oil and scatter with mint.

DRINKS, CAKES, CAVIAR, & CRÈME

THE SALTY FISH
& CAKES

FERNET OLD FASHIONED

A DRINK NAMED SUE

HONEY SYRUP

CHAMOMILE-INFUSED
HONEY SYRUP

A FIFTY-FIFTY

NIGHT OF THE COMET

THE GAME CHANGER

THE HEAD START

Drink pastis with water. Drink vermouth with Campari. Cold gin. Do a shot of hot gin if challenged to do so by Rustun Nichols, manager of the Ides and Reynard bar at the Wythe Hotel. Mix rye with bitters. Free pour your Negroni. Go easy. Go hard. Chartreuse and soda. Ice down the aquavit. Garnish in odd numbers. Stir the vermouth. A martini without vermouth is just a double.

This interlude is inspired by the early days of Diner. Whenever we offered a special menu at the restaurant, we would always start with drinks, potato pancakes, and caviar at the bar. Serving a bite of food alongside cocktails makes drinking feel quite elegant.

THE SALTY FISH & CAKES

Poor sturgeons, they grow slowly and mature late in life and many populations are very depleted or near extinction. We recommend caviar from reputable farmed fish in the United States or Canada. This makes 4 dozen silver dollar–sized potato pancakes. You might want more.

    4 large russet potatoes, peeled

    1 white onion, peeled

    1 egg, beaten

    Neutral oil (such as grapeseed)

    Kosher salt

    Crème fraîche, for dolloping

    2 ounces caviar (such as farmed United States beluga, osetra, or sevruga)

Grate the potatoes and onion on a box grater. Season with salt and pepper and toss to combine. By the handful, squeeze out as much liquid from the potato and onion mixture as possible and discard. Stir in the egg. Heat ¼ cup of neutral oil in a large skillet over medium heat. Once hot, drop several small spoonfuls of the potato and onion mixture into the skillet, being careful not to crowd the pan. Flatten each spoonful a bit. Fry until deeply golden, a couple of minutes on each side. Frying these pancakes is just as satisfying as eating them. Drain on paper towels. Season and top each pancake with a dollop of crème fraîche and a spoonful of caviar.

FERNET OLD FASHIONED

In honor of Fergus Henderson. In honor of the bees. In honor of a red nose and rosy cheeks and the stories they tell.

2 ounces rye

½ ounce Fernet-Branca

Scant ½ ounce honey syrup (page 83)

1 orange wedge, for garnish

Combine the rye, Fernet-Branca, and honey syrup in a mixing glass with ice. Stir until combined. The honey gives this drink a little cloud. Strain into a rocks glass over ice and garnish with the orange wedge.

A DRINK NAMED SUE

Every night at Roman's we run a sour and bitter cocktail special. For the bartenders, it can feel a little like cocktail roulette, depending on what spirits or kitchen ingredients we have on hand. We chose these ingredients because they were used as props in the Fernet Old-Fashioned photo, but also because I like to challenge Ryan Seaton, who tends bar at Roman's, with making something palatable from the absurd. Rain or shine, Ryan is always dressed for a funeral in June. The man in black, he never fails.

2 ounces Uno Blanco

½ ounce chamomile-infused honey syrup (page 83)

2 ounces freshly squeezed lemon juice

2 drops Amaro Dell' Erborista or any bitter, murky amaro

1 egg white

Dash of Peychaud's bitters

Chill a coupe glass in the freezer. Combine the Uno Blanco, honey syrup, lemon juice, amaro, and egg white in a cocktail shaker and shake hard for 10 seconds—without ice. This will fully incorporate your egg white. Add ice and shake again for 10 seconds. Strain into the chilled glass and let sit for a few seconds. The egg white will set up a little. Draw on the drink's surface with the bright red bitters, like an abstract painter.

HONEY SYRUP

1 jar honey

Eat a spoonful of honey to make a little room in your jar. Boil a kettle of water and stir as little as possible into your honey. Just enough to get it moving.

CHAMOMILE-INFUSED HONEY SYRUP

1 jar honey

1 chamomile tea bag

Eat another spoonful of honey from a different jar. Put the tea bag in a teapot. Boil a kettle of water, then add the boiling water to the teapot and let steep for about 4 minutes; you want the tea to be very strong but not creepy tasting. Once steeped, stir as little of the hot tea as possible into your honey, in order to get it moving.

A FIFTY-FIFTY

What I love about this drink is context. Our friend Shane Feirstein recommends this when you're not sure dinner is going to make it to the table in time, or ever. Take a moment to yourself. Don't worry about the shape of your ice. Ice melts. Drink fast.

Sweet vermouth

Club soda

1 lime wedge

Fill a tall glass with ice, then fill it halfway with vermouth. Pour in club soda to the top and squeeze in a lime. Drink in one gulp. For when it could go either way.

NIGHT OF THE COMET

This is a Corpse Reviver variation from Marlow & Sons bartender Josh Wiles. Josh has an affinity for the floral and a delicate sense of balance, physically and spiritually. Almost any cocktail could stand a little Cocchi Americano.

1 ounce Old Tom gin

1 ounce dry curaçao

1 ounce Cocchi Americano

1 ounce freshly squeezed lemon juice

1 maraschino cherry (optional)

Chill a coupe glass in the freezer. Combine the gin, curaçao, Cocchi Americano, and lemon juice in a cocktail shaker. Add ice and shake hard for 10 seconds. Strain into the chilled glass. Drop in a cherry if you have it. Wake the dead.

THE GAME CHANGER

———

It has to be fun. A night of service in a restaurant has to be fun. Working the grill station has to be fun. Writing the cookbook has to be fun. Doing the dishes has to be fun. If it's not fun, it's time to pack up and go home. Some nights, you can lose sight of this mantra. That's when you know it's time for the Game Changer. It's a drink with a purpose. This mood elevator comes our way via our friend Jim McHugh. It is blanco tequila or mezcal combined with green Chartreuse in a glass, as big or small as you need. "Tastes like the way a sun-warmed yard smells the morning after a bonfire," Jim says. At the bar we take our medicine in stages, first white then green.

1 shot blanco tequila or mezcal
1 shot green Chartreuse

Drink the tequila or mezcal, followed by the green Chartreuse. If you know how to blow fire, please do.

THE HEAD START

———

All of the best cocktails are variations on a theme. This duo was championed by Shane Feirstein while tending bar at Roman's. Tender is the night.

1 shot Fernet-Branca
1 shot Branca Menta

Drink the Fernet-Branca, followed by the Branca Menta. Rhubarb, saffron, midnight, and myrrh. Bitter, then menthol. Just what you need between now and never. Now and forever?

BÉA & THE PAELLA

FRIED TOAST *with* TOMATO

I ALMOST ALWAYS FAIL

RABBIT & CHORIZO PAELLA

CREMA CATALANA

Makes two pans for 16

We cook this every year for our daughter's birthday. Everyone gathers around the pan and eats with spoons. Wooden if possible. No plates. Burn the rice slightly if you can. In Spain, they call it *socarrat*. Allow your ingredients to carry you over land, sea, and scorched earth. Bomba rice is traditional but Kate likes Bhutanese red rice. Sometimes I add string beans or the long snaky beans I find in Chinatown, cut into short segments. This paella is made of rabbit, mussels, shrimp, squid, and dry chorizo, which releases a nice red paprika oil into the rice. Serve with aioli and enjoy the dramatic tension.

FRIED TOAST *with* TOMATO

This toast is fried, which creates an ideal texture for transforming the tomatoes. It could easily be grilled, if you want to stay outside by the fire.

Olive oil, for frying and drizzling

1 loaf country bread, cut into ½ inch slices

4 cloves garlic, peeled

4 large, ripe, juicy heirloom tomatoes, halved

Kosher salt

2 (7-ounce) jars, marinated white anchovies

Heat a generous amount of oil in a large sauté pan over medium heat until shimmering. Working in batches, fry the bread, swirling the pan and flipping the bread, until both sides are toasty and golden. Transfer the toast to a kitchen towel to drain. Continue to fry bread, adding more oil as needed. Rub each toast with garlic on one side, then rub with the halved tomatoes, sliced side down. The fried bread acts as a box grater, helping to crush the tomato into the toast. Season with salt and pepper and drizzle with olive oil. Top each toast with a school of anchovies.

I ALMOST ALWAYS FAIL

Aioli. Always aioli. The only time I get anxious is when I am making aioli; I think the garlic and oil can tell. I read once that, traditionally, Spanish grandmothers make aioli without egg; it's just a garlic and oil sauce. So every time I try it that way first, and I fail. I try it next with egg and fail. I go to the trouble. I never use a blender. And I usually even try to forgo the whisk. This process will, eventually, make about 3 cups.

3 cloves garlic

Kosher salt

2 cups olive oil

1 cup neutral oil

3 egg yolks (give the whites to your bartender)

Splash of water

½ lemon

With a large mortar and pestle, pound the garlic and a large pinch of salt into a paste. Stirring constantly, add 1 drop of oil. Then another. When you start to worry that it's not holding together, add an egg yolk and ask for help. This is when Scarlett Lindeman, our resident recipe editor, usually jumps in to save the day. Aioli is a confidence game. Continue adding drops of oil, very slowly, stirring all the while, until the garlic binds the oil and starts to thicken. You can add the oil in a stream now. Once you've added ½ cup of oil or so, you may need to add in a tiny splash of water to loosen the aioli up a bit before continuing. After you've incorporated 1 cup or so of oil, and the aioli threatens to cascade over the mortar, you can transfer it to a bowl and continue with a whisk and the rest of the oil. Taste. Squeeze in a bit of lemon juice, whisking well to combine, and season with more salt. Exhale. Aioli.

RABBIT & CHORIZO PAELLA

A paella pan is a necessity. The wide, flat shape of the pan aids in heating the rice evenly and coaxing your *socarrat*. You'll need two for this recipe. This is written for the ideal scenario, cooking outside on a wide grill, over open flames. You will need to manipulate your fire a bit here. When cooking on a stove top or on a typical backyard grill, you may want to halve the recipe, and regretfully the guest list.

3 onions, chopped

8 cloves garlic, minced

Olive oil

Kosher salt

1 tablespoon smoked paprika

1 teaspoon sweet paprika

Large pinch of saffron

1 (14½-ounce) can crushed tomatoes

2 tablespoons tomato paste

2 rabbits, broken down into legs, arms, and saddle

Kosher salt

4 cups short-grain rice (such as bomba or Valencia, even Bhutanese red rice)

Pitcher of water

2 (8-ounce) dry chorizo sausages, cut into ¼-inch slices

4 sprigs rosemary

8 ounces string beans, cut into short segments

8 ounces mussels, scrubbed clean

8 ounces large, head-on shrimp

4 ounces squid, cut into rings

Aioli, for serving (page 92)

Make the sofrito first; it can be done the day before. Gently cook the onions and garlic with oil and salt over low heat in a wide, heavy-bottomed pot. Cook it slow and low until the onions are truly soft; it will take at least an hour. Add the smoked and sweet paprikas and cook for a minute or two, stirring occasionally. Add the saffron, tomatoes, and tomato paste, mashing up the paste with a wooden spoon. Continue to cook the sofrito until it reaches a porridge consistency, about 15 minutes more. Cut the heat and reserve.

To cook the paella on a charcoal grill, get your fire going really hot, then let the coals burn down to medium-high heat. You don't want an active flame. You will know the coals are ready when you can hold your hand above them for a second or two without screaming. Alternatively, paella can be cooked on a gas grill or stove top over medium heat.

CONTINUED

Season the rabbit with salt. Pour 2 tablespoons of oil into each paella pan and brown the rabbit, transferring the rabbit pieces to a platter as they finish, about 10 minutes total. Divide the rice between the 2 pans and toast it in the fat over lower heat, moving the pans to the cooler part of the grill or lowering the heat slightly on your stove or gas grill. Add a bit more oil to coat the rice if it seems dry. Stir frequently. This should take a long time, up to 30 minutes.

When the rice starts to color and smells toasty, add half of the sofrito to each pan, stirring to combine. Add about 2 cups of water to each pan to get the rice saturated and moving. Return the pans to medium heat. Season well with salt, then place the rabbit and chorizo into the rice along with the rosemary. Sprinkle the string beans over the top. Bring the water to a simmer. Shift the pan around on the grill so the heat hits different parts of the pan, adding water when the pan starts to look dry or starts to smell scorched. Resist the urge to stir but do shuffle and shake the pan often. When the rice is just cooked through, 35 to 45 minutes, sink the mussels, shrimp, and squid into the paella and cook for a couple of minutes more, until the mussels open and the shrimp turn pink. Remove the pans from the heat and let sit, uncovered, for 10 minutes or so. Bring the pans to the table and serve with aioli and lots of spoons.

CREMA CATALANA

This recipe is courtesy of pastry chef Neale Holaday. Like another favorite of ours, the Spanish tortilla, dramatic tension in this recipe happens when you have to invert the custard, so make sure you have a plate big enough to cover for "the flip." We don't love corn syrup, but sometimes it's a necessity. Lyle's Golden Syrup, which can be found at most well-stocked supermarkets is a good alternative. This will make one 10-inch custard.

Grapeseed oil

1½ cups sugar

⅓ cup Lyle's Golden Syrup or light corn syrup

⅓ cup water

3 cups milk

¾ cup plus 2 tablespoons sugar

3 eggs

6 egg yolks (reserve whites for cocktails)

2 teaspoons vanilla extract

Find a pan that's large enough to fit the pot in which you will cook the caramel and prepare an ice bath in it. Find a large, round, ceramic baking dish and coat it with the grapeseed oil.

To make the caramel, in a heavy-bottomed pot, combine the sugar, Lyle's Golden Syrup, and water. Cook over medium heat, without stirring, until the sugar turns a nice amber color and smells toasty, about 10 minutes. Cut the heat and dunk the bottom of the pot into the ice bath for 10 seconds or so to stop the cooking. Pour the caramel into the prepared ceramic baking dish and let harden while you prepare the custard.

Find a roasting pan or baking dish that's large enough to fit the caramel-covered ceramic baking dish. Preheat the oven to 300°F. Boil a kettle of water.

Meanwhile, to make the custard, warm the milk and sugar in a pot over medium-low heat until the milk is hot and the sugar completely dissolves. In a large bowl, whisk together the eggs, egg yolks, and vanilla. Pour a splash of the hot milk mixture into the eggs, to temper them, whisking until combined. Whisk in another splash of the hot milk mixture, then pour the egg mixture into the milk, stirring to combine. Strain the custard. Pour into the caramel-covered dish and cover tightly with aluminum foil. Place the ceramic baking dish into the roasting pan and pour the hot water halfway up the sides of the custard-filled baking dish. Cover the roasting pan with aluminum foil. Bake the custard until just set, about 45 minutes, checking halfway through cooking. The center will be slightly jiggly. Remove the roasting pan from the oven, remove both covers of aluminum foil, and let cool completely.

When ready to serve, run a paring knife around the edge of the custard. Place a plate, upside down, over the ceramic baking dish, then confidently invert the baking dish and plate so that the custard unmolds from the baking dish and releases onto the plate. Serve on a flower-covered lawn.

A SUMMER FAREWELL

ADDIO ANTIPASTI

ROASTED OLIVES

TWO KINDS OF SPIRIT

MOREL TOAST

SALT-BAKED BRANZINO

RIB ROAST *with*
HORSERADISH

WATERCRESS *with*
MUSTARD DRESSING

HONEY PANNA COTTA
with SESAME TUILE

A party for 8 to 10

This menu is inspired by a series of dinners we have done for chefs when they've left our kitchens. Chefs work tirelessly in our restaurants, some hopefully staying on for years. When it's time for them to go—either for a new project or a new career—it's important to mark their time spent and acknowledge their efforts. Dinner can be a proper send-off and a way to create new experiences while also saying good-bye, thank you, and good luck.

ADDIO ANTIPASTI

Slice cured meats, prosciutto, finocchiona. Warm your olives. Pickle your vegetables.

6 leeks

1 head cauliflower, cut into florets

4½ cups distilled white vinegar

1½ cups water

3 tablespoons sugar

2 tablespoons kosher salt

2 teaspoons coriander seeds

1 teaspoon caraway seeds

1 teaspoon peppercorns

1 dried chile de árbol

Trim the roots off the leeks but leave the base intact. Trim the green tops from the leek and discard (or save in your freezer for stock on another day). Halve the leeks lengthwise and then cut each half into 3 long pieces. Rinse well in cold water and set aside leeks and cauliflower in a bowl. Bring the vinegar, water, sugar, salt, coriander, caraway, peppercorns, and chile de árbol to a simmer in a saucepan. Pour the pickling liquid over the vegetables. Cover and refrigerate at least overnight and up to 2 weeks. Serve the pickles with cured meats and warm olives while you finish cooking dinner.

ROASTED OLIVES

Olive oil

8 cloves garlic, unpeeled and smashed

3 sprigs rosemary

1 dried chile de árbol, crumbled

4 cups mixed olives, such as Castelvetrano, Kalamata, Cerignola, Gaeta, Niçoise, and Lucques

1 lemon

1 orange

Freshly ground pepper

Bay leaf

In a large, shallow pot, heat a generous pour of oil over medium heat. Add the garlic and toast until fragrant, just a minute or two. Add the rosemary and chile de árbol, then the olives. Lower the heat and stir to combine. Peel the lemon and orange rinds and throw them into the pot, then cut the lemon and orange in half and squeeze their juices over the olives. Add the bay leaf. Season with pepper. Warm the olives until heated through, about 10 minutes. The olives can be stored in the fridge in an airtight container for up to 2 weeks. Reheat gently before serving.

TWO KINDS OF SPIRIT

Let the booze be sweet. Let it flow, let it flow, let it flow.

3 cucumbers

½ cup lime juice

1 cup white rum

1 cup dark rum, like Goslings

1 cup Dolin Blanc vermouth

½ cup Velvet Falernum

A few cucumber rounds

To make cucumber juice, peel, seed, and chop the cucumbers. Blend and strain. You may need to add a splash of water to get the blender going. This will make a light but really green and flavorful juice. Juice your limes. Fill a pitcher with ice. Pour in the white rum, dark rum, vermouth, and Velvet Falernum. Add the cucumber and lime juice. Add as much ice as you can and stir with a wooden spoon. Toss in a few cucumber rounds.

MOREL TOAST

Only after you've spent hours in the woodland looking for wild mushrooms under every leaf—and only after finding one the size of your thumb—can you truly appreciate an abundance of wild mushrooms on a plate. We've served morel toast every spring at Marlow & Sons since Sean Rembold put it on the menu. It's a rite of passage, for mushroom season and for the young cooks just starting out in the kitchen.

2 pounds fresh morel mushrooms

8 tablespoons unsalted butter

2 tablespoons olive oil

3 large shallots, minced

1 small bunch thyme

Kosher salt and freshly ground pepper

Splash of white wine

4 cups heavy cream

1 round country bread, sliced

1 or 2 cloves garlic, peeled

1 bunch chives, chopped, for garnish

Brush the morels of any visible dirt and grit. Slice them in half. Gently wash them in cold water, then drain well. Taste a morel. If it's gritty, gently wash the morels again in more cold water until they're completely free of dirt. We typically do not wash mushrooms, but morels demand a good dousing. Dry them well on a kitchen towel.

In a large pot, melt the butter with the oil over medium heat. Add the shallots and sauté until translucent. Tie the thyme together with kitchen twine and toss it into the pot, along with the morels. Season well with salt and pepper and cook, stirring occasionally, until the morels start to release their liquid, about 10 minutes. Continue to cook until the mushroom liquid evaporates. Add the wine, stirring, and let it evaporate, too. Add the heavy cream and gently simmer until it has reduced a bit and nicely coats the morels, 5 to 10 minutes. Season with salt and pepper. Toast or grill the bread, then rub with a garlic clove on one side and spoon the morels over the top. Sprinkle with the chives.

SALT-BAKED BRANZINO

At some point in history, salt cost as much as gold. And now you can entomb a fish in it. A whole branzino or four in an igloo of salt.

- 4 (1½-pound) whole branzini, gutted and scaled
- 6 cups coarse salt
- ½ cup water, plus more as needed
- 2 egg whites, beaten until frothy
- 1 tablespoon fennel seeds
- 1 lemon, plus lemon wedges, for serving
- 1 bunch basil

Preheat the oven to 500°F. Rinse the fish and pat dry. In a bowl, combine the salt, water, egg whites, and fennel seeds. Zest the lemon into the bowl, then thinly slice it. Stuff the cavity of each fish with the lemon slices and basil. With your hands, mix the salt mixture until moist, like damp sand, adding a splash of water, if needed. Spread out one-third of the salt mixture on a baking sheet, forming it into a bed large enough to fit all of the fish. Place the fish on the salt and then cover them with the remaining salt mixture, pressing to seal the sides. The branzini should be completely covered with salt.

Roast for 20 minutes, then insert a paring knife through the salt into the center of a fish. Feel the tip of the knife. If it's warm, the fish is done. If it's cold, continue cooking, checking with your knife every 5 minutes, until the fish are done. Remove the baking sheet from the oven and let the fish sit in the salt for 10 minutes. Serve with a large knife or spoon and a bowl of lemon wedges. Allow your guests to crack and remove the salt until the fish is unearthed.

RIB ROAST *with* HORSERADISH

Horseradish sauce reminds me of taking over the reins at dinner. I would make horseradish sauce when I, as an adult, first started making dinner for special occasions. Sweet and spicy, it's an easy foil for any roast—and an excellent way to distract your guests if you happen to overcook the roast. Condiment and accomplice.

4 cups crème fraîche

2 tablespoons Dijon mustard

Juice of 1 lemon

2 teaspoons sherry vinegar

Kosher salt and freshly ground pepper

1 (6-inch) piece horseradish, peeled and chopped

1 (6-rib) standing beef rib roast, trimmed and tied by your butcher

To make the horseradish sauce, whisk together the crème fraîche, mustard, lemon juice, and vinegar. Season with salt and pepper. Pulse the fresh horseradish in a food processor until finely shredded, then whisk into the sauce. Refrigerate to let the flavors come together, at least a couple of hours and up to overnight. When ready to serve, strain through a fine-mesh sieve to remove any big bits of horseradish.

Remove the rib roast from the refrigerator and pat dry. Season the roast liberally with loads of salt and freshly cracked pepper. Let stand at room temperature for at least 1 hour to temper. Preheat the oven to 450°F. Set a roasting rack on top of a baking sheet and place the roast on it. Bake the roast for 20 minutes, then lower the oven to 350°F. The total cooking time will vary, depending on the weight of your roast—allow for around 15 minutes per pound. In about 2 hours, you'll have a juicy, rosy, rare to medium-rare roast. You can use an instant-read meat thermometer to determine if your roast is done to your liking. Personally, I prefer to stick a cake tester into the roast and press it against my lip, to be sure it's warm in the center. Build the suspense.

Let the roast stand in a warm part of the kitchen for 15 minutes, then cut away the kitchen twine and transfer the roast to a cutting board. Carve the ribs off the roast in one piece, then slice them into individual ribs. Carve the roast into ⅓-inch slices. Arrange the slices on a platter, with the ribs and any accumulated juices. Serve with the horseradish sauce on the side.

WATERCRESS *with* MUSTARD DRESSING

This Dijon dressing has a bite to it, which accentuates the bite of the greens. One bite begets another bite. Eye for an eye.

2 shallots, thinly sliced

½ cup sherry vinegar

Juice of 1 lemon

½ teaspoon dried oregano

Pinch of sugar

8 bunches watercress, washed and trimmed of woody stems

3 tablespoons Dijon mustard

1½ cups olive oil

Salt and freshly ground pepper

Combine the shallots, vinegar, lemon juice, oregano, and sugar in a large bowl. Let the shallots macerate for 10 minutes or so. Place the watercress in another bowl. Remove the shallots from the vinegar with a slotted spoon and sprinkle them over the watercress. Whisk the mustard into the vinegar mixture, then slowly add the oil, whisking until the dressing is emulsified. Season with salt and pepper. Dunk a sprig of watercress into the dressing and eat it. If it needs more kick, pour in a splash more vinegar. Adjust the seasoning, if necessary, then pour over watercress and shallots and toss.

HONEY PANNA COTTA
with SESAME TUILE

Panna cotta needs a foil—perhaps a little crunch or balsamic vinegar. Here, it's a cookie, or is it a tile or a wafer? In French, it's called a *tuile*.

4 cups heavy cream

3¼ teaspoons powdered gelatin

½ cup honey

1 teaspoon freshly ground pepper

½ teaspoon kosher salt

1 vanilla bean

4 tablespoons unsalted butter, at room temperature

½ cup confectioners' sugar

1 tablespoon honey

¼ cup egg whites

½ cup all-purpose flour, sifted

2 tablespoons untoasted sesame seeds

2 pints fresh blackberries

½ cup water

¼ cup granulated sugar

2 sprigs tarragon

Juice of 1 lemon

Put 1 cup of the cream in a medium saucepan. Sprinkle the gelatin over the cream and let sit for 5 minutes. Turn the heat to low and cook, stirring, until the gelatin completely dissolves. Stir in the remaining 3 cups cream, honey, pepper, and salt. Scrape the seeds from the vanilla bean and add both bean and seeds to the cream. Warm the mixture, stirring occasionally until the sugar dissolves. Strain through a fine-mesh sieve set over a bowl, then divide among 8 to 10 ramekins. Refrigerate until set, at least 4 hours.

Preheat the oven to 325°F. To make the tuiles, cream the butter and confectioners' sugar together until light and fluffy with an electric mixer, about 5 minutes. Add the honey and beat until combined. Add the egg whites, beating until just combined, then add the flour and beat until a smooth batter forms. Line a baking sheet with parchment paper. Spread the batter into 3-inch-wide, ⅛-inch-thick circles on the parchment paper. Sprinkle generously with the sesame seeds. Bake the tuiles until deep brown, 18 to 20 minutes, checking often. Remove from the oven and let cool completely, then peel from the paper. Break the tuiles into abstract shapes and store in an airtight container until ready to use.

For the blackberry sauce, crush the blackberries with the water, granulated sugar, and tarragon in a small pot. Bring to a boil, then simmer until the sauce has thickened slightly, about 5 minutes. Stir in the lemon juice, then strain the sauce through a fine-mesh sieve set over a bowl. Refrigerate until ready to use.

When ready to serve, pour 2 tablespoons of the blackberry sauce onto each plate. Run a paring knife around the edge of each panna cotta, then carefully invert it onto the plate. Top with a few pieces of the tuile.

I LOVE,
YOU LOVE,
WE ALL LOVE
BLUEFISH

Inspired by Ken Wiss, current chef of Diner and Marlow & Sons, as well as Caroline Fidanza, founding chef of Diner and Marlow & Sons, and all the people who enjoy and cook an undervalued fish. We first served this dinner in 2012, across the street from Diner in the dusty, gravel-filled parking lot. We set up a grill and tables, grabbed strangers, and invited them to sit down and eat. For the second seating, we served friends and family a large bluefish as the sun went down and all the tiny lights of New York City turned up. Bluefish is the unsung hero of the Northeastern sea.

BLUEFISH *with* ALMOND TARATOR

PLUM, PIMM'S, SPRITZ

PEPERONATA ON TOAST *with* LARDO

THE SQUID & THE FIRE-BLISTERED TOMATOES

GRILLED CORN *with* SHRIMP BUTTER

SHRIP BUTTER

EGGPLANT *with* BONE MARROW AGRODOLCE

LATER, A PITCHER OF MEZCAL & BITTERS

BERRY CROSTATA

A party for 8 to 10

BLUEFISH *with* ALMOND TARATOR

Bluefish comes in many shapes and sizes. A 2-pound fish for every two or three people will do.

6 slices of bread, crusts trimmed

2 cups milk

2 cup almonds, toasted

4 cloves garlic, smashed to a paste

8 tablespoons hazelnut or walnut oil

4 tablespoons red wine vinegar, plus more as needed

2 tablespoon honey, plus more as needed

Olive oil

Kosher salt

A school of 2-pound bluefish or several larger ones if you can find them, gutted and scaled

2 or 3 leeks

Lemon wedges

To make the tarator, soak the bread in the milk. After 5 minutes, squeeze the milk from the bread and place in a food processor; pulse with the almonds and garlic until a rough paste forms. Add the nut oil, vinegar, and honey, and pulse to combine. With the food processor running, pour in enough olive oil to form a smooth, spreadable sauce. Add a little water to thin it out, if necessary. Season with salt. Taste and add more honey or vinegar, if it needs it. The tarator should be garlicky, rich, and well balanced.

Bluefish tend to stick, so really scrub the grill to remove any residue. Oil a kitchen towel and rub down the grates. Get your grill hot. Brush the fish with olive oil and sprinkle liberally with salt. Wash the leeks and place them in the cavity of the fish. Place the bluefish on the hot grill. Cook for 8 to 10 minutes, then carefully flip it over. If the skin begins to stick and tear, cook the fish for another minute or two until it releases from the grill without sticking. Grill the fish on the other side, 6 to 8 minutes more. Insert a paring knife into the center of the fish. Feel the tip of the knife. If it's warm, it's done. If it's cold, continue cooking, checking with your knife every minute or two, until the fish are done. Serve the fish with the tarator sauce and lots of lemon wedges for squeezing.

PLUM, PIMM'S, SPRITZ

Plums have great style. Ruddy on the outside. Bright and sweet inside. This is a recipe for one. But no one really likes to drink alone, so multiply at will. The contagious cocktail.

2 plums, small and sweet

1 tablespoon freshly squeezed lemon juice

Pinch of sugar

1 ounce Pimm's No. 1

1 ounce Dorothy Parker gin

Dry sparkling wine

Fresh mint, if you've got it

Pit your plums, then muddle them in a mixing glass with the lemon juice and sugar. Add the Pimm's and gin. Add some ice and give it a good shake. Pour your drink into a glass. Add an ice cube or two and top off with sparkling wine. Stir so that your fruit doesn't get stuck at the bottom and serve. You could add mint to this. But then you could also spend the rest of the night making this drink, so be careful.

PEPERONATA ON TOAST
with LARDO

Lardo looks like marble but is actually the cured fatback from the pig. Sliced as thinly as possible, the fat will melt into any warm surface. Get it from your local butcher.

8 bell peppers (no green ones)

2 yellow onions

Olive oil

6 cloves garlic, peeled and smashed

Kosher salt and freshly ground pepper

Splash of white wine

Handful of fresh basil leaves

Handful of fresh mint leaves

Splash of sherry vinegar

20 slices country bread

16 ounces lardo, thinly sliced

Cut the bell peppers in half and remove the ribs and seeds. Dice the bell peppers and onions. Warm the oil in a wide, low-sided pot over medium-high heat. When the oil is quite hot, add the bell peppers, onions, and garlic and season with plenty of salt and pepper. The vegetables will release a fair amount of liquid, so stir and continue to cook them until they soften and start to caramelize, about 25 minutes. Deglaze the pan by adding the wine and scraping up any browned bits at the bottom of the pot, allowing the wine to evaporate. Toss in the basil and mint, add the vinegar, and stir to combine. Cut the heat and let the flavors mingle at room temperature for 30 minutes. When the peperonata has cooled a bit, taste and season with more salt and pepper, if necessary.

Toast the bread on the grill until crusty and charred. If you don't feel like using a grill, toast the bread in a broiler or toaster. When ready to serve, top the toast with the lardo and spoon the peperonata on the toast and top with the lardo.

THE SQUID & THE
FIRE-BLISTERED TOMATOES

Braising the squid over the wood fire really makes a difference in this recipe. Cook outside. Take it to the streets or the backyard.

8 large, ripe heirloom tomatoes

Olive oil

6 cloves garlic, smashed to a paste

1 fresh cayenne pepper, slit down the middle, with seeds

1 bunch thyme

2 bay leaves

Kosher salt and freshly ground pepper

3 pounds squid, cleaned and sliced (page 209)

1 bunch parsley, chopped

Country bread, sliced and charred on the grill

Get a grill going hot, then allow the coals to burn down to medium heat. Alternatively, you can set your gas grill at a low temperature.

To make the tomato sauce, rub the tomatoes with a little oil and place them on the grill. Every so often, flip or move the tomatoes around. Ideally, they won't burst but roast within their skin. Grill the tomatoes until tender and cooked through, 30 minutes or more, then transfer them to a pot suitable for braising on the grill and let cool. When the tomatoes are cool enough to touch, break them up with your hands. Place the pot directly on the grill and add the garlic and cayenne, with its seeds. Tie the thyme together with kitchen twine and toss it and the 2 bay leaves into the pot. Season with salt and pepper and add some olive oil. Bring the tomato sauce to a low simmer.

Season the squid with salt and pepper and add to the tomato sauce, stirring to combine. The squid will tense up, then become rubbery after a few minutes. Cook until the squid is tender again, 30 to 40 minutes. Stir in the parsley at the last minute and serve with lots of grilled bread to soak up the sauce.

GRILLED CORN *with* SHRIMP BUTTER

Sean Rembold blew our minds one summer when he fried corn and poured green onion and shrimp butter over it. On the grill this also picks up a nice smoke.

20 ears sweet corn, left in their husks

1 pound Shrimp Butter (see recipe below)

1 pound shrimp, peeled, shells reserved

10 green onions, thinly sliced

Kosher salt

Get a grill going hot. Grill the corn in their husks, turning occasionally to cook evenly. The husks will char and crumble away, but the kernels will steam-roast inside, remaining sweet and juicy. Remove the corn from the grill after 25 to 30 minutes. Let sit for 5 minutes, then peel off the husks and corn silk. Warm the shrimp butter in a saucepan on the grill. Dice the shrimp, then gently poach them in the shrimp butter for a minute or two, just until opaque. Break the corn cobs in half and place in a large bowl. Spoon the shrimp and shrimp butter over the corn, then toss in the green onions. Season well with salt and toss well. Get messy.

SHRIMP BUTTER

This butter comes dressed like a John Hughes movie, pretty in pink.

1 pound unsalted butter

Shells from 1 pound of shrimp

1 shallot, minced

1 tablespoon brandy

2 teaspoons kosher salt

Put the butter and shrimp shells in a saucepan over low heat. Tamp down the shells with a rolling pin to crush them slightly. Add the shallot, brandy, and salt. Let the butter melt and steep over very low heat, stirring occasionally, for about 1 hour. The shells will start to infuse the butter with shrimp flavor, and the butter will become clear as the milk solids sink to the bottom of the pan and turn pink. After 1 hour, strain the butter through a fine-mesh sieve lined with cheesecloth set over a large bowl. Discard the shells and other solids. Return the butter to a small saucepan and keep warm.

EGGPLANT *with* BONE MARROW AGRODOLCE

Marrow bones are behind the counter at every butcher shop. Your butcher can cut the bones into short segments, making the marrow easy to access. Steeped in the agrodolce, the marrow will melt into the sauce, adding fat and richness to the sharp vinaigrette. Don't be afraid. Cook with bones.

4 pounds of beef marrow bones, cut into 4-inch segments

Kosher salt and freshly ground black pepper

3 cloves garlic, peeled and crushed

1½ cups sugar

¼ cup water

1¼ cups sherry vinegar

Pinch of red pepper flakes

12 baby eggplants, halved lengthwise

Handful of fresh basil leaves, torn

An hour or two before cooking, soak the marrowbones in really salty ice water, which will help draw out any residual blood or impurities from the bones.

To make the bone marrow agrodolce, preheat the oven to 300°F. Put the bones on a sheet tray and season with salt. Bake until the marrow is soft and gelatinous, about 15 minutes. Scoop the marrow from the bones with a small spoon and place it in a small pot with the garlic. Once cool, give the bones to your dog. Over low heat, toast the garlic in the marrow until golden and fragrant, about 5 minutes. Set aside.

In a medium pot, combine the sugar and water; it should be the consistency of damp sand. Cook the sugar mixture over medium-high heat. The sugar will caramelize and turn lightly golden brown, then darker, until it reaches a nice auburn color. At this moment, cut the heat and add the vinegar. It will spatter and spit violently. It's agro rearing its head, so be careful. Bring the caramel back to a simmer over medium heat, stirring to combine the caramel and vinegar. Add the marrow and garlic mixture, stirring to combine. Add the red pepper flakes and season with salt and pepper. Keep warm until ready to serve.

On a charcoal grill, get your fire going really hot, then let the coals burn down to medium-high heat. Place the eggplant, cut side down, on the grill and cook until charred and softened, 5 to 7 minutes per side. As soon as it comes off of the grill, season with salt and black pepper. Arrange on a platter, spoon the marrow agrodolce over the top, and sprinkle with the basil.

LATER, A PITCHER OF MEZCAL & BITTERS

We recommend drinking many cans of icy cold beer with bluefish. However, a cocktail in the middle of a party is never a bad idea. Especially a strong one. If you can find Unión Mezcal, buy it. Our friend Champion makes it. It's smooth and smoky and balances brightly with bitters.

3 or 4 cane or raw sugar cubes

The ubiquitous Angostura bitters

Club soda

1 bottle mezcal

Ice

1 orange

1 lemon

Toss the sugar cubes into a pitcher. Douse them with bitters. Add a little club soda, then muddle the sugar and bitters until the sugar dissolves. Pour most of your bottle of mezcal into the pitcher, leaving room at the top. The drink will mix as you build it. Top off the pitcher with ice. Garnish with twists of lemon and orange for a little color. Eat the orange. Save the lemon for squeezing on the bluefish.

BERRY CROSTATA

Free-form fruit tart. This recipe makes 3 pounds of dough, enough for two 11-inch pastries.

5 cups all-purpose flour

3 tablespoons granulated sugar

1 tablespoon kosher salt

1 pound unsalted butter, cut into 1-inch cubes and chilled

¾ to 1 cup very cold ice water

3 pounds fresh assorted berries, such as raspberries, blueberries, blackberries, or hulled and sliced strawberries

½ cup granulated sugar

2 tablespoons brandy

1 egg white, beaten

2 tablespoons turbinado sugar

Vanilla ice cream, to accompany

A day before you bake the crostata, whisk together the flour, granulated sugar, and salt in a medium bowl. Using a pastry cutter or 2 knives, cut the butter into the flour mixture until the butter is the size of small peas, working quickly. Sprinkle ¾ cup of the ice water slowly and evenly over the flour-butter mixture, stirring to combine. The dough should just come together. Test it by pressing a small bit together with your fingertips; it should stick together well. If it crumbles apart, sprinkle more ice water over the top and lightly combine with your hands. Test again with your fingertips. The amount of water needed can vary depending on the weather. Divide the dough in half, quickly pack each half into a ball, and place on a large piece of plastic wrap. Compress each ball tightly with the plastic wrap. Then with a rolling pin, roll the dough into a compact disk. Repeat with the second ball of dough. Refrigerate overnight. The next day, pull the dough from the refrigerator. Let it sit at room temperature for 10 minutes, then roll into two ⅛-inch thick circles. Transfer each dough circle to a parchment-lined baking sheet; they will overhang before you fold them around the berries. Don't panic.

To make the filling, toss the berries gently with the ½ cup granulated sugar in a large bowl. Crush a fistful of the berries with your hand, then add the brandy and fold everything together. Immediately arrange the fruit on the rolled-out dough, making sure to leave a 3-inch border at the edges. Fold the dough border over the berries, pleating the edges. Refrigerate the crostata until cold, about 20 minutes to an hour.

Preheat the oven to 400°F. Brush the dough with the egg white and dust with the turbinado sugar. Bake until golden, gently lifting the tarts with a large spatula to check that the underside is golden as well, about 30 minutes. Let cool, then cut into wedges and serve with ice cream.

THE TOMATO & THE SEA

PURPLE PICKLED EGGS

FRIED CALAMARI SANDWICH

PANZANELLA

Serves all

When you have already considered enough . . . Tomato, mayonnaise, salt. Prosciutto, butter on bread. You don't need a recipe, just enjoy. Then consider packing it all up and go to the sea. Sit on the dock of the bay. Call it a day. The endless summer. This is not quite a menu. Just a collection of a few of our favorite things.

PURPLE PICKLED EGGS

This is like dyeing your clothes, but it's an egg. The eggs take on the color of the beet in just an hour or so, pale and pink, getting darker and more deeply dyed as they sit. After 24 hours, you'll have a bright magenta egg.

12 eggs

1 red beet, peeled and chopped

4 cups distilled white vinegar

1 cup water

Handful of sugar

Smaller handful of salt

3 sprigs tarragon

Prepare an ice bath. Bring a pot of water to a boil, then slip in the eggs and cook for 7½ minutes. Transfer the eggs to the ice bath. When cool enough to touch, crack the shells and return them to the ice bath, submerging them until cooled, about 10 minutes or so.

Meanwhile, in a medium pot, bring the beet, vinegar, water, sugar, and salt to a boil. Cut the heat and let the pickling liquid cool to room temperature. Peel the eggs and submerge the eggs along with the tarragon in the pickling liquid. Refrigerate in an airtight container until ready to use, preferably overnight. When ready to serve, slice in half and finish with a dash of salt.

FRIED CALAMARI SANDWICH

I'm still not sure why this sandwich tastes as good as it does. I imagine that this style of sandwich is served in every outdoor cafe on the Mediterranean coast, on flimsy tasteless rolls and even sometimes without aioli—just bread and perfectly fried squid. This recipe will make four loaded sandwiches.

12 ounces fresh squid, cleaned and cut into ¼-inch rings (page 209)

Grapeseed oil cut with a little olive oil, for frying

2 cups semolina flour

2 tablespoons finely ground cornmeal

1 tablespoon kosher salt

4 crusty rolls

½ cup aioli (page 92), again, the never-ending story of the never-ending aioli

Lemon wedges, for serving

Have your squid prepped and ready. Heat a fryer or a sturdy, shallow pot with 2 inches of oil until 350°F. Whisk together the semolina, cornmeal, and salt in a shallow bowl. If you don't have a frying thermometer, test the oil temperature by dredging a ring of squid in the semolina mixture, shaking off any excess, and dropping it into the oil. The oil should bubble up and the squid should rise to the top, but not violently (turn the heat down) or lackadaisically (turn the heat up)—just a nice bubbly bubble. Dredge the squid ringlets in the semolina mixture, tossing them about with your hands to coat well, then shake off any excess and slip into the hot oil. Fry the squid until very crunchy and starting to turn pale golden, 1 to 2 minutes. Pull the squid from the oil with a fine-mesh strainer and transfer to a bowl. Toss the squid with the salt. Cut the rolls in half, then slather both sides of the rolls with aioli. Pile the calamari onto the rolls and serve, lemon wedges on the side.

PANZANELLA

This is a good use of a tomato, the juice and the whole of it—everything but the stem. Aim for balance—the sweetness of super-ripe tomatoes, the acidity of red wine vinegar, the grassiness of the herbs. This is a savory something that's refreshing in the middle of summer. This panzanella will satisfy four.

½ loaf country bread

Olive oil

2 cloves garlic, smashed to a paste

Kosher salt

4 ripe, juicy heirloom tomatoes

2 small cucumbers

1 small red or white onion, thinly sliced

2 tablespoons capers, rinsed and chopped

5 sprigs marjoram

1 small bunch basil, leaves picked

⅓ cup red wine vinegar

Freshly ground pepper

Preheat the oven to 350°F. Slice crust off bread and tear into pieces. In a large bowl, toss the bread with oil, garlic paste, and salt, massaging everything together so the bread soaks up the oil and the garlic paste is evenly distributed. Spread out the pieces of bread on a baking sheet and bake until they start to color and the edges crisp up, stirring occasionally, about 15 minutes. Let the bread cool to room temperature. The bread pieces will firm up as they cool: you don't want them to be rock-hard; there can be pieces with give.

Cut the tomatoes into irregular bite-size wedges. If the cucumbers' skin is bitter, peel the cucumbers before slicing into similarly interesting bite-size wedges. In a medium bowl, combine the tomatoes, cucumbers, onion, and capers. Pull the marjoram leaves from their stems, then coarsely chop them. Add the marjoram to the bowl along with the basil leaves, tearing any large ones as you go. Add the vinegar and oil, season well with salt and pepper, and toss to combine. Check the seasoning and add in a bit more salt or vinegar, if necessary. Add the bread to the bowl and toss everything together. Let the panzanella sit for about 5 minutes before serving. We like the bread crunchy.

AFTERNOON AROUND THE FIRE

YOGURT TAHINI

GARLIC SAUCE

FETA *with* CHILES & HERBS

PUFF THE MAGIC PITA

BABA GHANOUSH

GRILLED, BLITZED-UP CHILES

FREEKEH *with* WALNUTS
& HERBS

SPATCHCOCK CHICKEN

DATES, ALMONDS, & COCONUT

Enough for 12

Scarlett Lindeman, the recipe editor for *Diner Journal*, and I always joke about starting a chicken restaurant. It's really only funny in its absurd simplicity. Before restaurants, there are just ideas. There is a certain spontaneity to this menu. It's the kind of thing you can easily pull together while you work on other things. But it proves to be no less satisfying than all the dinners you planned and worked meticulously on. As Scarlett puts it, "A meal can come together languidly because of a spark that happened long ago. Some flavors stay with you, they lodge inside your mind, and you can resurrect and conjure them at will. Grilled chicken stained with spice. Garlic sauce. It can all come together in an afternoon with friends. Swirl together some yogurt and tahini, roughly mash a couple eggplants, pick herbs for a grain salad, grill a handful of chiles, and there you have it. Even if you don't ace the flavors, by then you will realize it's really about the process, the scene, the setting, and the setting sun."

YOGURT TAHINI

Two condiments walk into a bar … I like a ratio of 4-to-1 yogurt to tahini, swirled together so you can still see tan and white streaks.

3 cups thick yogurt, homemade if you've been paying attention (page 62)

½ cup tahini

Kosher salt

Stir everything together in a bowl with a spatula. Do not go all the way.

GARLIC SAUCE

Be a detective. Be inspired by a flavor. Be in pursuit of your *own* recipe. If a flavor stays with you, try and figure it out. The secret here is potato, which binds and thickens the sauce.

1 small russet potato

1 head garlic, separated and peeled

Kosher salt

⅓ cup freshly squeezed lemon juice

1 cup neutral oil (such as grapeseed)

¼ cup good olive oil

Wrap the potato in foil and roast in the coals while your chickens cook. When cooked, cut in half and scoop out its fluffy insides. Discard the skin. With a large mortar and pestle, pound the garlic and salt into a paste. Transfer the garlic paste to a food processor. Add the lemon juice and 2 tablespoons of the potato and pulse to combine. With the blender running, slowly add drops of the neutral oil, blending all the while, until a creamy, smooth sauce forms. If the sauce seems a bit too runny, add in another tablespoon of the potato and process until thickened. Eat the rest of the potato while no one is looking. Add the olive oil in a thin stream, to finish. Season well with salt. Refrigerate and let the flavors mingle for 30 minutes or so. Taste and season with salt, if needed. The sauce should be aggressively garlicky, lemony, and not too thick.

FETA *with* CHILES & HERBS

Squares and circles. Floating flowers.

4 packages good feta, cut horizontally into ½-inch-thick slices

1 bunch oregano

1 bunch thyme

1 bunch mint

1 small bunch chives, with flowers if possible

1 whole cayenne pepper, thinly sliced

1 lemon

Olive oil

Freshly ground black pepper

Place the feta on a high-sided platter. Pick the oregano, thyme, and mint leaves from their stems and scatter over the feta. Pick the chive flowers and chop the chives, then scatter the flowers and chopped chives over the feta along with the cayenne pepper. Zest the lemon over the top, then drizzle with oil. Season with black pepper. Let sit at room temperature for a couple of hours.

PUFF THE MAGIC PITA

Try to make these balls of dough puff up like balloons on the grill. It's a good challenge because it doesn't always happen. The magic of steam. The pitas can also be cooked in a ripping-hot cast-iron pan.

1¾ cups lukewarm water

2½ teaspoons active dry yeast

Pinch of sugar

3 cups all-purpose flour, plus a bit more for surface dusting

1 cup whole wheat flour

2 tablespoons olive oil, plus more as needed

2 teaspoons kosher salt

In a large bowl, stir together the water, yeast, and sugar. Let the yeast bloom for 5 minutes. Add the flours, oil, and salt. With your hands, mix the dough until all the flour has been incorporated and the dough gathers into a ball. It will be really sticky. Continue to work the dough against sides of the bowl, kneading and turning, until it is smooth and elastic. After 10 full minutes of kneading, the dough will become less sticky and more homogenous. Transfer the dough to a well-oiled bowl and let sit at room temperature, covered with a kitchen towel, for about 2 hours. It should roughly double in size.

Punch down the dough. Divide into 12 pieces with your hands and roll each piece into a compact, smooth ball. Rub each one with a little oil, place on a flat surface, and cover with a kitchen towel. Let the dough rest at room temperature for 30 more minutes. On a lightly floured surface, roll each ball into a ¼-inch-thick disk with a rolling pin or an empty bottle of mezcal.

On a hot grill, grill each pita for a minute or two on each side. The pitas should puff up and inflate. Let them get a little char before flipping and cooking the other side. Brush the pita with oil and eat it hot. Burn your fingertips if you can stand it, but do be wary of the hot steam.

BABA GHANOUSH

Ode to the nightshade, slightly poisonous, but we eat eggplant anyway. Grill and smoke the impenetrable purple vegetable; you can even burn it. Andrew says luscious. Kate says sensuous. Anna says, coy daddy, pampered papa, father of the pestle.

4 large purple Italian eggplants

½ cup tahini

2 cloves garlic

Juice of 2 lemons

Olive oil

Kosher salt

Get your grill ripping hot, then let the coals burn down a bit. Roast the eggplants over open coals until charred and collapsing. Transfer the charred eggplant to a bowl and cover with a kitchen towel to steam. When cool enough to touch, peel off the blackened skin; it's fine if some flecks remain. Mash with a whisk. A whisk is nice because it leaves some texture. Add the tahini, then microplane the garlic into the bowl. Add the lemon juice, oil, and salt, whisking until a rough mash forms. Let the flavors get to second base at room temperature. This can take an hour or two. Adjust the seasoning, top with some more olive oil, and serve.

GRILLED, BLITZED-UP CHILES

This is not a recipe. This is what you do with peppers. When shopping for chiles, look for a blend of varieties and spice levels. It's always nice to have some red ones in there for color. Though certain varieties are sure to be spicier, the level of heat really varies from pepper to pepper—it can feel a bit like playing farmers' market roulette.

Assorted fresh chiles, such as ají dulce, pasilla, hot cherry, red jalapeño, serrano, cayenne, and random heirloom varieties

Olive oil

Kosher salt

Grill lots of hot chiles until blistered and charred, then let cool completely. Remove their stems and most of their seeds. Pulse in a blender with a bit of oil and salt until you get a loose salsa. Don't inhale. Taste with caution.

FREEKEH *with* WALNUTS & HERBS

Freekeh is an ancient grain that doesn't get starchy like spelt does. More than anything else, this is a choose-your-own-adventure recipe. Feel free to use different nuts, herbs, or greens. Just keep watermelon out of the mix. Unless it's a watermelon radish, which might be nice.

4 cups freekeh

2 cup walnuts, toasted and chopped

1 bunch spinach, trimmed

1 bunch parsley, leaves plucked

1 bunch mint, leaves plucked

1 large handful dried apricots, diced

1 large orange

Olive oil

Juice of 1 lemon

Kosher salt and freshly ground pepper

Cook the freekeh in plenty of boiling, salted water until tender, about 30 minutes. Drain well. Let cool before tossing with the walnuts, spinach, parsley, mint, and apricots in a large bowl. Zest the orange over the top, then add the oil and lemon juice. Cut the orange in half and squeeze its juice into the bowl. Season well with salt and pepper. Toss and taste. Let the flavors meld at room temperature for an hour or so.

SPATCHCOCK CHICKEN

When grilling a chicken, I like to spatchcock it. Just remove the backbone by cutting along its edges, then flatten the chicken like a textbook you're pretending to read.

10 cloves garlic, peeled

⅓ cup freshly squeezed lemon juice

1 tablespoon dried thyme

2 tablespoons sweet paprika

1 tablespoon ground cayenne pepper

1 tablespoon kosher salt, plus more to season

1 teaspoon freshly ground black pepper, plus more to season

¼ cup olive oil

4 (2½-pound) chickens, spatchcocked

Blitz everything but the chickens in a blender or a food processor until a paste forms. Rub the spice paste all over the chickens, coating them evenly. Refrigerate overnight. Pull the chickens from the refrigerator 1 hour before you plan to eat them. Season again with salt and pepper.

Get a grill going hot, then let the coals die down to medium. Grill the chickens, breast side up, shuffling them around on the grill to avoid any flare-ups, about 20 minutes. Flip the chickens and continue to grill, rotating them around the grill so that they cook evenly, until they are nicely charred, about 20 minutes more. To check for doneness, prick one of the chicken thighs close to the bone to see if the juices run clear. A slight pinkish hue is fine; they will continue cooking as they rest. Transfer the chickens to a platter, breast side up so the skin stays crispy, and let rest for 10 minutes before serving.

DATES, ALMONDS, & COCONUT

So good, they deserve a coy name. Hide the nut? Almonds make a date? The double date?

1 or 2 almonds for every date

Olive oil

Kosher salt

2 cups shredded, unsweetened coconut

2 cups dates

Preheat the oven to 350°F. Toast the almonds on a baking sheet until fragrant, about 10 minutes. DO NOT BURN THE NUTS!!!! Remove the almonds from the oven, toss with a tiny splash of olive oil, and season well with salt. Set aside.

Spread out the coconut on another baking sheet and toast in the oven, just a minute or two. Slice open the dates and remove their pits. Turn them inside out so the outside is sticky, then stuff each date with 1 or 2 almonds. Wrap the date around the nuts and squeeze to seal. Roll each inverted, stuffed date in the coconut, pressing to adhere. Make one, eat one. Make two, eat one. Repeat.

UNDER THE HARVEST MOON

SWEET CORN ARANCINI

GREEN GAZPACHO

ROASTED FENNEL *with* FRIED QUINOA

EGGPLANT GRATIN

SHELL BEANS

SHORTCAKE *with* SUGAR PEACHES

Serves 6 to 8

This menu, originally written by Ken Wiss, the chef at Diner and Marlow & Sons, is inspired by years of us traveling upstate to do dinners with Guy Jones of Blooming Hill Farm. Over the years, Guy has taught us to *Never Buy Food from Strangers* and encouraged us to live like legends. We thought it would be nice to do this dinner for another farmer and her family, Patty Gentry of Early Girl Farm. Patty has taught us to be thankful for all we have around us and to nurture plants and people alike. Listen to your farmers. Eat vegetables for dinner.

SWEET CORN ARANCINI

Arancini can feel like a lot of work for just two bites, but it's worth it. A little bite of something fried is always a nice way to start a dinner, especially a vegetarian one.

12 ears sweet corn, shucked

Kosher salt and freshly ground pepper

Olive oil

1 onion, finely chopped

2 cups Arborio rice

Pinch of saffron

Splash of white wine

3 to 4 cups water

½ cup grated Parmigiano-Reggiano

Juice of ½ lemon

8 ounces fresh mozzarella, cut into ½-inch cubes

All-purpose flour

2 eggs, beaten

4 cups panko bread crumbs

Neutral oil (such as grapeseed)

Put a small bowl upside down inside a larger bowl. Rest the base of a corn cob on the small bowl and slice off the kernels with a knife. Continue slicing the kernels off the cobs until they're all kernel-free. Set aside. In another bowl, scrape each cob with the back of a knife to release the corn milk. Combine the corn milk with an equal amount of raw kernels in a blender and puree, adding just enough water to get the blender moving. Season with salt and pepper. Strain the corn mixture through a fine-mesh sieve, reserving the strained liquid to cook into the risotto; you should have around a cup. Discard the solids. Sear the remaining corn kernels in a sauté pan with a splash of olive oil very briefly, just a minute or two, until they plump ever so slightly. Season with salt and pepper. Set aside.

In a medium-sized pan, sweat the onion in a bit of olive oil until soft, about 5 minutes. Season with salt and pepper, add the rice and saffron, and cook, stirring often, until the rice is toasted, about 10 minutes more. Deglaze the pan by adding the wine and scraping up any browned bits at the bottom. Cook until the wine evaporates. Add the water, 1 cup at a time, stirring until it's absorbed by the rice and the rice is almost cooked, about 15 minutes. Finally, add the corn milk, stirring well until it's absorbed by the rice. The risotto should be thick but not stiff. Fold in the seared kernels and the Parmigiano-Reggiano, followed by the lemon juice to brighten. Adjust the risotto seasoning and spread it out on a baking sheet lined with parchment paper. Refrigerate until completely cool.

To assemble the arancini, form golf ball–sized balls of risotto around pieces of mozzarella. Place the flour, beaten egg, and bread crumbs in separate shallow bowls. Roll each risotto ball in the flour, dip in the egg, then coat with the bread crumbs. In a sturdy, shallow pot, heat 2 inches of the neutral oil until it's 350°F. Deep-fry the risotto balls in batches until golden, 3 to 4 minutes each. Scoop them from the oil with a spider strainer. Drain the arancini on paper towels. Serve warm.

GREEN GAZPACHO

When you're going to eat on the farm, consider preparing the vegetables raw in order to appreciate their natural sweetness and flavors.

8 large or 12 small cucumbers, peeled and seeded

Juice from 2 limes

Olive oil

Kosher salt and freshly ground pepper

1 cup mint leaves

1 cup cilantro leaves

1 cup tarragon leaves

1 cup dill leaves

2 cups almonds, soaked overnight in water, plus ⅓ cup unsoaked, for garnish

2 cloves garlic

1 tablespoon sherry vinegar

1 wedge honeydew melon, rind removed and seeded

2 cups homemade yogurt (page 62)

Thinly slice the cucumbers and place in a large bowl. Toss with the lime juice and oil and season with salt and pepper. Add the mint, cilantro, tarragon, and dill, then toss and let sit at room temperature for an hour or so. The marinade will start to break down the cucumber, loosening it up. Working in batches, puree the cucumber mixture and the soaked almonds in a blender with the garlic and sherry vinegar, on high, adding a splash of olive oil to each batch. Strain the mixture through a fine-mesh sieve set over a bowl. Refrigerate until chilled, about 1 hour.

Preheat the oven to 350°F, toast the unsoaked almonds for 10 minutes until fragrant. Finely chop the almonds and in a bowl combine with ¼ cup oil and season well with salt. Dice the melon into small cubes. When ready to serve, whisk the gazpacho well, taste it, and adjust the seasoning. Garnish with the chopped almonds, cubed melon, and dollops of yogurt and a drizzle of olive oil.

ROASTED FENNEL *with* FRIED QUINOA

The day before serving cook your quinoa, spread it on a baking sheet and leave in the refrigerator overnight. This will dry it out. Frying quinoa transforms the now ubiquitous grain into a crackling, crunchy afternoon delight. This is your grain on drugs.

12 bulbs fennel, stalks and fronds removed

Olive oil

Kosher salt and freshly ground pepper

4 cups quinoa, cooked and dried

4 cups cherry tomatoes

1 clove garlic, smashed to a paste with salt

1 bunch chives, chopped

2 cups aioli (page 92)

Cut the fennel bulbs into ½-inch-thick wedges and cut away as much core as you can without fully removing it; you want the wedges to stay intact. Toss with a healthy dose of olive oil and season with salt and pepper. Get a grill going hot, then let the coals die down to medium-hot. Grill the fennel until charred and just tender, about 15 minutes. Transfer to a baking sheet and let cool to room temperature.

In a sturdy, shallow pot, heat an inch of the olive oil until it's 350°F. Deep-fry half the quinoa until it starts to change color, about 30 seconds. Use a fine-mesh strainer to scoop the quinoa from the oil and let cool on a baking sheet lined with parchment paper. Repeat with the remaining quinoa. Cut the cherry tomatoes in half and toss in a bowl with a bit of olive oil, garlic paste, and the chives. Season with salt and pepper. When ready to serve, spread the aioli on a large platter and arrange the roasted fennel on top. Pour the tomatoes and their liquid over the fennel and sprinkle the fried quinoa on top.

EGGPLANT GRATIN

4 large purple eggplants

Kosher salt

Olive oil

2 small bunches rosemary

1 small bunch thyme

4 or 5 cloves garlic, unpeeled

3 bay leaves

Juice of 1 lemon

2 pounds green beans, trimmed

2 cups cherry tomatoes

1 teaspoon dried oregano

1 bunch basil, leaves picked

Freshly ground black pepper

½ cup grated Parmigiano-Reggiano

2 cups ricotta cheese, at room temperature

2 cups toasted bread crumbs (page 23)

1 red chile, such as cayenne or red jalapeño, sliced

1 bunch marjoram, leaves picked

1 tablespoon balsamic vinegar

Cut the eggplant in half lengthwise. Score the cut sides of the eggplant and sprinkle with salt. Let drain in a colander in the sink for an hour. Preheat the oven to 350°F. In a skillet, cook the eggplant sliced side down in a glug of oil until brown, about 8 minutes, then transfer to a baking sheet. Scatter the rosemary, thyme, garlic, and bay leaf among the eggplant halves and bake until the eggplant is cooked through, about 30 minutes. Let cool to room temperature, then scoop the eggplant out of its skin. It's all right if some is mushy and some is firm, hopefully all of it is oily. Discard the rosemary, thyme, garlic, and bay leaves. Season with salt and lemon juice. Turn on your oven's broiler.

Meanwhile, char the green beans, dry, on a grill or under a broiler until quite black on the outside. If you do it fast and hard, the beans should keep some of their texture, though the outside may have ashy skin. Run a knife through the beans so they're more or less cut in half, widthwise. Set the green beans aside. Blister the tomatoes in a dry sauté pan under the broiler, then add oil, season with salt and pepper, and cook just until the tomatoes pop, about 5 minutes.

Combine the eggplant, string beans, tomatoes, dried oregano, and basil in a large bowl. Season with salt, pepper, and a bit more oil and fold in the Parmigiano-Reggiano. Taste the eggplant mixture; it should be well seasoned.

To assemble the gratin, spoon the eggplant mixture into a large baking pan or individual gratin dishes. Dollop spoonfuls of ricotta cheese on top and then sprinkle bread crumbs over the whole thing. Bake just until warm and the bread crumbs look good and crusty, about 30 minutes. Sprinkle the sliced chile, picked marjoram, and black pepper over the top. Drizzle with the balsamic vinegar and olive oil to finish. Serve hot, warm, or at room temperature.

SHELL BEANS

Fresh shell beans are incomparable. Whichever kind—cannellini, cranberry, pinto—late-summer shell beans are worth the meditation time they take to shuck. When cooking outside, we set a pot of them in the corner of the fire pit for a slow-burning, lengthy dish. At home on the stove, they should take about an hour.

10 cups shell beans (such as cannellini, cranberry, or pinto), shucked

2 carrots

1 rib celery

1 large white onion

3 sprigs sage

Handful of garlic cloves, peeled

2 glugs olive oil, plus some of the good stuff for drizzling

Small handful of kosher salt

Place the shell beans in a large pot and add enough cold water to just cover. Snap the carrots and celery in half and add them to the pot. Slice the onion in half and add it to the pot, along with the sage and garlic. Pour the oil over the top. Bring the shell beans to a gentle simmer, skimming off any froth that rises to the surface and stirring occasionally. Cook until they are just tender, about an hour. You should be able to easily crush a bean between your forefinger and thumb. Add the salt. Remove the pot from the heat and let the beans sit for at least an hour. When ready to serve, taste the beans and their liquid and adjust the seasoning. Spoon into a large bowl and drizzle with good olive oil.

SHORTCAKE *with* SUGAR PEACHES

Neale Holaday provided this shortcake recipe. This makes eight shortcakes and works well with any fruit that's in season.

1¾ cups all-purpose flour

½ cup cake flour

4 teaspoons granulated sugar

1½ tablespoons baking powder

1 teaspoon salt

8 tablespoons unsalted butter, cut into cubes and chilled

14 tablespoons buttermilk

Splash of heavy cream

2 tablespoons turbinado sugar

Coarse sea salt

8 peaches, the juiciest, ripest ones you can find

2 tablespoons granulated sugar

3 cups heavy cream

¼ vanilla bean

To make the shortcakes, preheat the oven to 375°F and line a baking sheet with parchment paper. Whisk together the all-purpose flour, cake flour, granulated sugar, baking powder, and salt in a large bowl. Using your hands, work the butter into the flour mixture until the butter is the size of small peas. Stir in the buttermilk until just combined. Pack the dough into a compact lump and transfer to a lightly floured work surface. Roll out the dough until it's 1 to 1½ inches thick. With 3-inch round cutters, cut out 8 shortcakes and transfer to the baking sheet. Brush the shortcakes with the heavy cream and sprinkle with turbinado sugar and a pinch of sea salt. Bake until golden brown, 18 to 20 minutes. Let the shortcakes cool to room temperature.

Cut the peaches into 1-inch thick wedges, toss with the granulated sugar, and let sit for about 30 minutes before serving. Then whip the cream with the seeds scraped from the vanilla bean. Cut the shortcakes in half horizontally. Spoon the peaches and their juices and a dollop of whipped cream on top of the shortcake bottoms, then crown with the shortcake top hats.

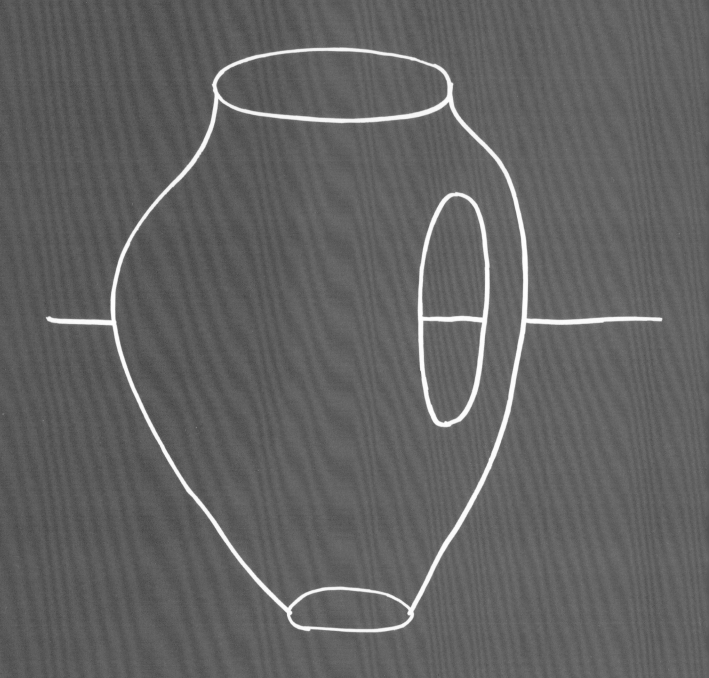

BON
ANNIVERSAIRE

THE BASE
OF BOUILLABAISSE

THE BUOY
OF BOUILLABAISSE

ROUILLE, MEANING RUST

TAPENADE

SQUID & SAFFRON

A FALLING GREEN

FRUIT AS AN ILLUSION

A pot for 16

What is it to look at a photograph in a book and long to participate? Read a recipe from the hillside of coastal France and try to recreate it? Nostalgia for a life we haven't lived? Empathy? Jealousy? Something about exceeding our natural limitations, our physical boundaries?

This dinner came out of reading and romanticizing Richard Olney's book *Lulu's Provençal Table*, and later, Alice Waters. We wanted to live in Provence and drink Bandol rosé, have access to all the best ingredients, cook in a place with a tradition as rich as its soil.

The place on Long Island where we recreated the dinner couldn't have been farther from southern France. But by the time the sun set that mid-July day and the sky became that dusky blue, we were all engulfed in rosé. Kate and I cleaned monkfish, then rubbed them with saffron and olive oil. We were celebrating our wedding anniversary. Another dimension, marriage. A circle of sea, a pot of stuff. The porthole. Kate's dress was translucent green like the shimmering flesh of the fish.

THE BASE OF BOUILLABAISSE

Stock. Nuance. Scum. The three funny words I hear as I tend to my post, skimming the bouillabaisse. The stock can be made, refrigerated, and stored up to three days before serving. It is good for any kind of fish soup, small or grand, though this is a grand recipe. You'll need a big pot to fit three heads and spines from any large, non-oily fish. The carcass of any 5-dollar fish will do.

Olive oil

3 leeks, cleaned and trimmed, cut in half

3 bulbs fennel, quartered, with fronds

4 red onions, quartered

6 ribs celery, halved

6 carrots, halved

6 cloves garlic, peeled

6 ripe small tomatoes, quartered

2 tablespoons tomato paste

3 sprigs thyme

2 teaspoons fennel seeds

2 bay leaves

1 dried chile de árbol, crumbled

Pinch of saffron

1 (750-milliliter) bottle dry white wine

Peel of 1 orange

3 fish carcasses, gills removed and bones broken into manageable portions

3 (1-pound) whole porgies, sea breams, or other mild whitefish, gutted, and gills removed

12 live green crabs (p.s. no need to clean the crabs and never Google "how to clean crabs")

Kosher salt

In a large pot, warm the oil over medium heat and add the leeks, fennel and fronds, onions, celery, carrots, and garlic and cook, stirring occasionally. After 30 minutes or so, the vegetables will start to brown and caramelize. Be careful not to let them scorch. Add the tomatoes, tomato paste, thyme, fennel seeds, bay leaves, chile, and saffron and stir well, breaking up the tomato paste and scraping up any browned bits at the bottom of the pot. Cook for another 15 minutes. Pour a gulp of wine out for the crabs you will kill, then dump in the rest of the bottle. Add the orange peel, fish carcasses, and porgies. Add enough cold water to cover and bring to a lively boil. Drop in the live crabs, one by one, making sure each one is fully submerged before adding the next. Once the crabs are no longer moving, lower the heat and simmer for an hour. Skim the scum that rises to the top diligently. This is the nice, relaxing part. Have a pastis. Skim often. Make the scum removal your sole purpose. Simmer, with one bubble rising to the top at a time, for another hour or two. Look for the stock to congeal. A thin skin should form on the surface of your stock.

CONTINUED

Once the stock has been at it for a couple of hours, fish out what solid matter you can with tongs, including the crabs, and discard. Pour the stock through a strainer set over a large pot to remove the remaining solids, then strain again through a strainer lined with cheesecloth. Taste the stock. It should be rich and flavorful. If it seems a bit wan, boil it for 30 minutes or so to reduce it and concentrate the flavors. Season with salt. Refrigerate until ready to use.

The day you'll serve the bouillabaisse, bring your stock to a bare simmer in the large, handsome pot you'd like to serve it in. Taste the stock once warm; it should be well seasoned. The seasoning here is not about saltiness; the ocean is already in the stock. Does the stock feel round and complete? When the stock is ready, it will be enriching and take on a soft red hue.

THE BUOY OF BOUILLABAISSE

If the weather is nice and you have the ambition and the grill, the soup can be warmed over a wood flame. I've even heard rumors of putting a small ember in the bouillabaisse to enhance the flavor with a little char and smoke. I love the simplicity of poaching the fish in the stock. You can really use whatever mix of fish looks good at the market, but it is important to consider cooking times, such as who goes first and who goes last. Tougher fish first, gentle fish later, shellfish finally.

4 gallons bouillabaisse stock (page 199)

1 pound monkfish fillets, cut into 2-inch pieces

1 eel, gutted and skinned, cut into 2-inch pieces

3 whole porgies, sea bream, or other mild whitefish, filleted and cut into 3-inch pieces

1 small whole butterfish for every guest, gutted and scaled

2 pounds mussels, scrubbed clean

2 pounds squid, cleaned (page 209) and sliced into 1-inch rings

Kosher salt

4 cups rouille (page 205)

2 loaves country bread, sliced and toasted

In a large pot, heat the stock to a low simmer. Add the fish and other shellfish and gently poach. Start with the monkfish and eel, five minutes later, drop in the porgies and butterfish, 5 minutes after that, the quick-cooking mussels and squid, which will only take a minute or two. Taste the stock and adjust the seasoning . Slather the rouille on the toasted bread. Carry the pot to the table. Divide the bouillabaisse among individual bowls, with 1 butterfish and a mix of monkfish, porgy, eel, mussels, and squid in each one. Float a rouille-covered toast on top of each serving.

ROUILLE, MEANING RUST

For me, rouille is the most complicated aspect of this dinner, which may be due to my lack of affinity for binding oil and garlic together. Challenging but necessary. Rouille is the orange lifeboat in the sea of bouillabaisse. This will make about 4 cups.

⅓ cup torn pieces of crustless country bread

2 large pinches of saffron

½ cup bouillabaisse stock (page 199), at room temperature or chilled

3 cloves garlic, peeled

Many pinches of kosher salt

5 egg yolks

1 lemon, halved

2 cups olive oil

2 cups neutral oil (such as grapeseed)

In a small bowl, soak the bread and saffron in the stock until soft. With a large mortar and pestle, pound the garlic and a large pinch of salt into a paste. Add the egg yolks, stirring to incorporate. Squeeze the juice from a lemon half with your hand, catching any seeds in the process, then stir to incorporate. Gather the softened bread and wring out as much stock as you can, reserving it in the bowl for later. Be sure to really wring the bread out. You only want the essence of the stock to be in the rouille. Add the bread to the mortar, pounding it until combined.

It's time to emulsify, so think congealing thoughts. Combine the olive and neutral oil into a cup with a spout. Have a friend slowly drip the oil into the mortar to start. Go very slowly at first, adding just a couple of drops of oil while rapidly stirring with the pestle. Keep stirring. Add a couple more drops of oil. Keep stirring. Pour in a thin stream of oil, stirring all the while. Stop pouring every now and again to make sure the rouille is emulsifying properly.

The rouille will start to thicken; sprinkle in a splash of the reserved stock to loosen it up. Continue pouring in a thin stream of oil, alternating with splashes of stock when the rouille gets very thick. If your mortar is too small and you can't stir vigorously without it cascading over the sides, transfer the rouille to a bowl and use a whisk. Squeeze the juice from the remaining lemon half into the rouille. Season with salt. Taste the rouille. Let it sit for a while for the flavors to meld. Just before serving, taste and adjust the seasoning.

TAPENADE

Use a mix of olives, with different colors and textures. The tapenade should look like a canopy of green. Salty and briny, serve this with bread before your soup. Eat the herbs.

1 cup salt-packed capers

4 cups mixed pitted olives, such as Castelvetrano, Kalamata, Cerignola, Gaeta, Niçoise, and Lucques

Leaves of 6 small sprigs oregano

Leaves of 4 sprigs thyme

1½ cups olive oil

3 cloves garlic, smashed to a paste

1 tablespoon white wine vinegar

1 teaspoon red pepper flakes

Zest of 1 lemon

Zest of 1 orange and ½ its juice

1 teaspoon freshly ground black pepper

1 loaf country-style bread, sliced

Rinse the capers thoroughly. If you don't have salt-packed capers, you can use brined ones, just be sure to drain and rinse them. Chop the capers and olives finely with the oregano and thyme and transfer to a bowl. Stir in the oil, garlic paste, vinegar, red pepper flakes, lemon and orange zests, orange juice, and black pepper until well combined. Taste. The tapenade should taste quite sharp. If it's too salty, add a splash of oil. Toast the bread under a broiler or on a grill. Serve with the tapenade.

SQUID & SAFFRON

If you don't know how to clean a squid, just ask a friend. Someone like Millicent Souris, who grew up plucking and rinsing them in the back of her family's saloon. If you do know, teach someone else. Either way, it's good to have company. Or alternatively ask your fishmonger to clean the squid for you. Cleaning and cooking squid can feel like handling the alien.

2 pounds squid

3 cloves garlic, smashed to a paste

Large pinch of saffron

Kosher salt

Olive oil

Coarse sea salt

Handful of fennel fronds, minced

1 lemon, cut into wedges

To clean the squid, place it lengthwise on your cutting board and prepare an ice bath. Cut the squid just below the eye to remove the tentacles from the body. There will be a hard node at the center of the tentacles; remove it. Drop the tentacles into the ice bath. Reach inside the tube-shaped body and remove the head, guts, and most important, a hard, plastic-like bit that is the backbone. Drop the cleaned, empty body into the ice bath and discard everything else. Rinse the squid, then drain well. Repeat with the remaining squid. If the squid are large, you can slice the bodies and tentacles in half.

Get a grill ripping hot. In a bowl, toss the squid with the garlic, saffron, and salt. Though squid swim around in saltwater, their flesh is not inherently salty. They need some. Add a good pour of oil to the mix. When the grill is so hot that you can barely hold your hand over it, drape the squid bodies and tentacles on the grates. Don't overcrowd the grill. Resist the urge to fiddle with the squid. Just leave them alone to char, which will only take a minute or two. As soon as the squid turn opaque, transfer them to a platter. Douse with more oil, a bit of crunchy salt, and the fennel fronds. Serve with lemon wedges.

A FALLING GREEN

As summer becomes fall, the season for delicate heads of lettuce ends and the darker, sturdier greens take over. It's hard to get excited about kale, unless you're attending a lesbian potluck. Ease your way in. You can catch the brief overlap of the two, when crispy lettuces and more toothsome greens can cavort in one salad. The herbs are important here, too—not supporting cast members but stars.

> 2 bunches baby red Russian kale
>
> 4 endives, sliced into 1-inch ribbons
>
> 3 heads radicchio, leaves plucked
>
> 2 bunches early fall lacinato kale or dandelion greens, leaves torn
>
> 1 lemon, halved
>
> Sea salt
>
> Olive oil, for drizzling
>
> 1 bunch parsley, leaves picked from their stems
>
> Handful of chives, sliced into batons
>
> Small handful of mint leaves

In a large bowl, gather together the mix of early fall greens. Squeeze the lemon juice all over the leaves, then season with sea salt, tossing to combine. Drizzle oil over the greens. Toss the greens, giving them a gentle massage with your fingers, especially the more sturdy greens. Add the parsley, chives, and mint and fluff the salad with open hands. Taste a leaf or two, then adjust the seasoning. Eat with your fingers. Discover paper cuts.

FRUIT AS AN ILLUSION

Choose pears that are just shy of juicy ripeness, and firm enough to withstand a little cooking. The poached fruit will be whole, pristine, but once you slide a fork into it, its transformed state is revealed. Form and function. Serve the pears in small bowls with some of their cooking liquid and a selection of your favorite cheese and crackers.

  3 pounds Seckel pears

  1 (750-milliliter) bottle white wine

  1¼ cups sugar

  1 cup water

  1 teaspoon fennel seeds

  Peel and juice of 1 lemon

  1 teaspoon kosher salt

Peel the pears, leaving the stems intact, which will help the pears retain their shape. Combine the pears, wine, sugar, water, fennel seeds, lemon peel, and salt in a pan. Simmer until the pears can be pierced easily with a paring knife, about 15 minutes. Stir in the lemon juice. These poached pears can hold up to a week if stored in their cooking liquid.

RIBOLLITA &
READINESS

BEANS, WAKE UP

RIBOLLITA

CARROT CUES, *with*
PISTACHIO & PARSLEY

BROCCOLI RABE,
OLIVES, CITRUS

HASSELBACK APPLE CAKE

A soup for 6 to 8

Ribollita is a pleasure to make. Tending to the pot, watching and waiting as the flavors develop, is so satisfying. Color. Aroma. Readiness. Ribollita may be made from humble ingredients. With a little attention, vegetables, beans, and day-old bread can develop into a revelation. When we first wrote about it in the *Diner Journal* we were looking to write a long-form recipe, something contemplative and expansive that might evoke Elizabeth David.

> *"Ribollita is a conversation between you and your dinner and it will give back what you give to it. To me, dishes like this are all about love and the belief that food can make you feel connected to something wonderful and basic, huge and intimate. Dinner can do all of this."*
> —Caroline Fidanza

BEANS, WAKE UP

Beans can be considered fussy, but aren't we all after waking from a deep sleep? Dried beans are asleep. You will reawaken them. Sometimes they're done in an hour and a half and other times they take three. That's why it's smart to cook the beans before you start the ribollita.

1 pound dried cranberry, borlotti, or cannellini beans

12 cups water

1 small bunch thyme

1 small bunch sage

6 bay leaves

1 head garlic

¼ cup olive oil

Kosher salt

Soak the beans overnight in plenty of water. If you have time, it's even better if you can soak them for 2 days. Just make sure they're in the refrigerator for the second day.

Drain and rinse the beans through a colander. Put the beans in a large pot, ideally one that is wide rather than tall. Add the water. Bring to a boil, then reduce to a simmer—you don't want these beans bumping into each other. Tie the thyme and sage together with kitchen twine and toss them into the pot along with the bay leaves. Slice the head of garlic in half lengthwise and add it to the pot. Add the oil and enjoy the way it pools on top of the beans. With a ladle, skim the surface of any froth that rises. Gently simmer until the beans are just tender. (You can also slide the pot of beans into a 325°F oven, with a lid; just don't forget about them.)

The cooking time will vary from 45 minutes to 2 hours, based on the soaking time and general freshness of the beans. Once the beans start to swell, which can happen anywhere from 30 minutes to an hour, start tasting them at frequent intervals. When they taste exactly as you would want them to if you were going to eat them right then, add salt. Cut the heat and let the beans soak up the seasoned cooking liquid as they cool.

RIBOLLITA

If Elizabeth David were writing this recipe, it would be short, indeed, because in many ways it is a short recipe with a long cooking time. You could probably read *Introduction to French Country Cooking* in its entirety in the amount of time it takes for this soup to cook.

"Good food is always trouble and its preparation should be regarded as a labour of love."
—Elizabeth David

Olive oil

2 Spanish onions, diced

8 cloves garlic, sliced

Salt, salt, salt

2 large carrots, diced

6 ribs celery, diced

1 bunch parsley leaves, coarsely chopped

2 (28-ounce) cans whole tomatoes

1 small head savoy cabbage, chopped

1 bunch lacinato kale, chopped

1 pound beans, cooked (page 218)

1 loaf crusty Italian-style bread, torn into 1 inch pieces and toasted until golden

In a large cast-iron pot or Dutch oven, warm the olive oil and add the onions, garlic, and a good amount of salt. Sauté over high heat until the onions start to release their liquid, about 5 minutes. Add the carrots, celery, and a pinch of salt, lower the heat to medium, and continue to cook. If at any point the vegetables start to look dry, add a little more olive oil. Stir regularly. You want the vegetables to move around in the pot; you don't want them to stick. After about 30 minutes, they should have softened a bit and are maybe even getting a little golden. Add the parsley and cook for another 5 minutes.

Open the cans of tomatoes and crush them with your hands, then add the tomatoes with their juices to the pot. Keep one of the cans nearby. Add another large pinch of salt and simmer the tomato and vegetable mixture for 30 minutes. Stir regularly. Add the cabbage and kale to the pot and a tomato can full of water. Stir and cook for another 30 minutes.

CONTINUED

Pull out the herbs and garlic from your beans. Pour off the beans' cooking liquid and reserve. Add three-quarters of the cooked beans to the soup along with a cup of their cooking liquid. Puree the remaining beans with some of their liquid to create a thick slurry and add them to the soup. Stir until well combined, then add 4 cups of water to the pot. Simmer over low heat for 1½ hours. From time to time, check to be sure that the beans aren't sticking to the bottom of the pot. The flavor will deepen as you cook. One thing is certain, you want to cook out the red color of the tomatoes and the bright green of the cabbage and kale. The soup will begin to take on a rust color and that's when you know it's just about done.

Check the seasoning again. If it seems like the soup needs a lot of salt its because you are essentially cooking vegetables and water. Salt will help the flavors develop and come together. When the ribollita is done, add the bread, stir it around well, and let it absorb the liquid and begin to fall apart, about 5 minutes. Serve the ribollita in bowls, drizzled with oil.

CARROT CUES, *with* PISTACHIO & PARSLEY

This is a salad of spontaneous shape and flavor. Always eat it with your fingers. Always add a nut to a salad. Always taste your carrots. If they are woody, consider making something else.

1½ pounds carrots of every color

1 bunch parsley, leaves pulled from stems

2 handfuls shelled pistachios, toasted and coarsely chopped

1 shallot, thinly sliced

Red wine vinegar

Juice of ½ lemon

Kosher salt

Freshly ground black pepper

Olive oil

With a vegetable peeler, shave the carrots into ribbons, until you cannot peel them anymore. Take what is left from each carrot and stick it in your refrigerator for a snack or to save for a soup. Put the carrot ribbons in a large bowl and add the parsley, pistachios, and shallot. Sprinkle with vinegar and lemon juice and season with salt and pepper. Dress with the oil, then toss the salad with your hands. Juggle the ingredients together until well coated. Hide the utensils.

BROCCOLI RABE, OLIVES, CITRUS

An unlikely trinity. Bitter, briny, and sweet. This medley is as much a meditation in texture as it is in flavor.

2 bunches baby broccoli rabe, more buds and leaves than stems

Olive oil, for drizzling

Kosher salt

4 tangerines

2 oranges (your standard navel)

Pinch of red pepper flakes

Freshly ground pepper

½ cup green olives, pitted

A handful of arugula

Heat the broccoli rabe in a dry grill pan over medium heat until the leaves crisp up and the stems get a good char, about 8 minutes. Transfer to a plate, drizzle with oil, and season with salt. Chop into 3-inch portions. Peel the tangerines and oranges with a knife, being careful to remove as little of their flesh as possible. Cut off any stray bits of pith, then slice them into ¼-inch rounds. Scatter the orange slices on a large platter, then season with the salt, red pepper flakes, and pepper. Scatter the olives, arugula, and the broccoli rabe on top. Douse with good olive oil.

HASSELBACK APPLE CAKE

Hasselback technique is most often done with potatoes, but here the cinnamony lemon juice drips down into the grooves cut into the apples. This cake is great for breakfast the next day.

10 tablespoons unsalted butter, at room temperature, plus more for greasing

3 tiny apples, peeled, halved, and cored

1 tablespoon freshly squeezed lemon juice

2 tablespoons light brown sugar

6 tablespoons granulated sugar

2 tablespoons, plus ¼ cup honey

2 teaspoons vanilla extract

3 eggs, yolks and whites separated

1 cup plus 2 tablespoons all-purpose flour

2 teaspoons baking powder

½ teaspoon kosher salt

1 tablespoon freshly squeezed orange juice

Coarse sea salt

½ cup heavy cream, beaten to soft peaks

Preheat the oven to 350°F. Grease a 9-inch springform pan with butter, then line the bottom of the pan with a round of parchment paper and grease the paper as well. Place the apple halves, cut side down, on a cutting board. Use a knife to cut halfway through the apple halves in thin parallel slices, so that they stay intact. This is hasselbacking. In a bowl, toss the apples with the lemon juice and the light brown sugar.

Beat together the butter and granulated sugar in a bowl with an electric mixer until fluffy, about 5 minutes. Add the 2 tablespoons of honey and beat until combined. Add the vanilla and egg yolks, beating until just combined. Sift together the flour, baking powder, and kosher salt in a small bowl. Fold the flour mixture into the butter-sugar mixture until just combined.

In another bowl with clean beaters, beat the egg whites until stiff peaks form, about 5 minutes. With a rubber spatula, stir half of the egg whites into the batter, then gently fold in the remaining egg whites until just combined. Pour the batter into the prepared cake pan, smoothing the top. Arrange the apple halves, flat side down, onto the cake batter, pressing them down slightly. Pour the accumulated apple juices onto the cake. Bake until a toothpick or cake tester inserted into the center of the cake comes out clean, 35 to 40 minutes.

Let cool on a rack for 5 minutes, then slide a knife around the edge of the cake and remove the sides of the springform pan. Let the cake cool completely.

When ready to serve, make a glaze in a small pot by warming the remaining ¼ cup honey with the orange juice and whisking together until loose. Brush the honey mixture all over the cake and sprinkle with the coarse sea salt. Serve with the whipped cream.

CARRY THE SPICES HOME

LAMB TAJINE

COUSCOUS *with*
PINE NUTS & CURRANTS

CUMIN & CORIANDER
PUMPKIN SEEDS

GRILLED FLATBREAD

PICKLED CARROTS

PAUL BOWLES OF YOGURT

APRICOTS IN HONEY

MINT TISANE

A tajine for 6 to 8

Search for exotic spices. Carry them home in your pockets. A good tajine will be sweet and earthy. Cook it slowly. Perfume the house. Matisse. Romance. Moroccan sun. Serve tajine with no utensils on the table. Only bread, lamb, yogurt, and pickles. Another dinner named after a vessel. Still life.

LAMB TAJINE

A tajine typically has a sloping triangular-shaped lid with a hole at the top that traps condensation and returns it to your stew. If you don't have a proper tajine, a heavy pot with a tight-fitting lid and a fitted piece of parchment paper will do.

4 tablespoon unsalted butter, at room temperature

1 tablespoon kosher salt

2 teaspoons ground ginger

2 teaspoons ground cumin

1 teaspoon ground turmeric

Large pinch of saffron

2 cloves garlic, smashed to a paste with salt

2 pounds lamb shoulder, neck, or leg (boneless is good, bone-in even better), cut into large cubes

Olive oil

7 yellow onions, thinly sliced

Kosher salt

2 teaspoons ground cumin

2 teaspoons ground coriander

1 teaspoon freshly ground pepper

1 cup lamb or chicken stock or water

1 (2- to 3-pound) sweet winter squash, such as sweet dumpling or red kuri, 1 half peeled, seeded, and cut into 2-inch cubes (keep the other half for another use)

Here's the rub. Made of butter and vibrant spices, this rub is fragrant and bright, like inky yellow paint. The butter is a necessary fat—lamb is a lean animal. In a large bowl, stir together the butter, salt, ginger, cumin, turmeric, saffron, and garlic until well incorporated. Add the lamb and massage the spiced butter into the lamb, making sure to cover all of it well. Once your lamb is nicely coated, you can cover and refrigerate it overnight or proceed with the recipe.

Preheat the oven to 300°F. Heat the oil in a tajine or heavy pot over medium heat. Add the onions, season well with salt, and sweat until the onions release their liquid, about 20 minutes. Add the cumin, coriander, and pepper, stirring to let the spices bloom for about 10 minutes. This is the fragrance. Add the lamb, with all of its buttery rub, and the stock and bring to a simmer.

If you're not using a traditional tajine, cut out a parchment paper round that's the circumference of your pot and tear a nickel-size hole in its center. Place on top of the simmering stew. Cover the tajine or pot and slide it into the oven. Bake for 2 hours, then carefully remove the lid and parchment, if using. Add the squash, re-cover the tajine or pot, and bake for 1 more hour. Let cool at room temperature for 30 minutes. Just before serving, adjust the seasoning. Put the tajine in the center of the table, within reach of everyone.

COUSCOUS *with* PINE NUTS & CURRANTS

I dream of a couscoussier. Maybe I just like saying the word *couscoussier*. With tajine, I will often make this plain. The flavors of the lamb are so developed I think of unadorned couscous as the perfect foil. With the addition of pine nuts and currants, this can stand on its own.

4 cups water	2 teaspoons koser salt
¼ cup olive oil	Pinch of ground cardamom
2 tablespoons unsalted butter	3 cups couscous
¾ cup pine nuts	½ cup currants
1 shallot, minced	1 bunch parsley leaves, chopped

Bring the water to a boil in a pot on the stove. In a medium saucepan, heat the oil over medium heat. Add the butter, and pine nuts and toast the pine nuts in the fat, stirring often, until they smell fragrant, just a couple of minutes. Add the shallot and cook for a minute, then add the salt, cardamom, and couscous. Stir well. Pour in the 4 cups of boiling water, cut the heat, cover the pot, and let sit for 10 minutes. Fluff the couscous with a fork. Really fluff it up. Make sure there are no clumps sticking together. You want it loose. Season with salt, then stir in the currants and parsley.

CUMIN & CORIANDER PUMPKIN SEEDS

These seeds are nice to have around. Good in salads, floated onto soups, or eaten by the handful while the tajine works its magic.

1 large egg white	¼ teaspoon ground allspice
½ teaspoon chili powder	¼ cup sugar
1 teaspoon ground cumin	1 teaspoon kosher salt
1 teaspoon ground coriander	1½ cups shelled pumpkin seeds

CONTINUED

Preheat the oven to 300°F. Grease a rimmed baking sheet. In a bowl, beat together the egg white, chili powder, cumin, coriander, and allspice until soft and foamy, about 2 minutes. Add the sugar, salt, and pumpkin seeds and stir until the pumpkin seeds are well coated. Spread out the seeds in a single layer on the prepared baking sheet. Bake until fragrant and starting to turn color, about 15 minutes, stirring occasionally. Remove from the oven and let cool completely.

GRILLED FLATBREAD

Expect that you and everyone you know will want to eat this right off the grill. Make more than you think you'd ever need.

1 tablespoon active dry yeast

2½ cups lukewarm water

6 cups all-purpose flour

3 tablespoons olive oil, plus more for brushing

4 teaspoons kosher salt, plus more

Za'atar

Activate the yeast in the water until frothy. Add flour, oil, and salt. Mix until all flour is incorporated then let sit out for an hour. Knead the dough until smooth. It will be sticky. Place in a well-oiled bowl that is significantly larger than the dough. It will expand. Cover tightly with plastic wrap and refrigerate overnight.

The next day, turn the dough onto a lightly floured surface. Divide into 15 pieces. Cover with plastic wrap and let rise for 30 minutes, or an hour if the room is cold.

Get a grill going hot, allowing the flames to go down. Stretch each piece of dough out with your hands as if you were working the graveyard shift at your local pizzeria. Gently let gravity to do your work. Aim for a uniform ½ inch thickness with a vaguely oval shape, though each flatbread will have its own unique curves. Drape the dough onto the grill, flipping when the first side is firm and charred, about 3 to 5 minutes total. Brush with oil and sprinkle with salt and za'atar. Repeat with the remaining dough. Stack the flatbreads like books. You will have enough dough to serve about 15 flatbreads, give or take a few, depending on how many are eaten right off the grill.

PICKLED CARROTS

Pickles will add a little brightness to the beginning of your dinner, figuratively and literally. I like to simmer the carrots for a hot minute or two in the pickling liquid. They lose some of their snappy rawness and give a little more.

8 ounces red, purple, and/or yellow carrots

3 cups distilled white vinegar

¾ cup water

Handful of salt

Smaller handful of sugar

2 teaspoons black peppercorns

Wash the carrots well and scrub them with a kitchen towel. No need to peel them. Cut the carrots on the diagonal into ¼-inch slices. In a pot, bring the vinegar, water, salt, sugar, and peppercorns to a boil. Add the carrots and simmer for 2 minutes. Transfer the carrots and the pickling liquid to an airtight container and refrigerate at least overnight. The longer they sit, the better they get. They peak at about a week.

PAUL BOWLES OF YOGURT

A bowl of yogurt should find its way to any table; it works with almost anything. Yogurt, bread, and honey. Yogurt, olive oil, herbs, and lemon. Yogurt, garlic, and spice. You can drain off some of liquid if you like, by straining it, and collecting the yogurt when it is as thick as you want it. To cultivate a culture of your own, see recipe on page 62.

APRICOTS IN HONEY

Hot water is regenerative, not just to cranky humans but also to dried fruit, dried chiles, and tea leaves. Nonsulfured apricots are brown and are preferred for this dessert. These apricots are also great over yogurt for breakfast. End the day. Begin the day.

2 cups honey

1½ cups water

1 pound dried apricots

1 cup dried plums

1 cinnamon stick

1 star anise

1 teaspoon black peppercorns

Pinch of kosher salt

Combine all of the ingredients in a pot. Bring to a boil, then lower the heat and simmer for 5 minutes. Cut the heat and let steep, covered, until ready to serve. Refrigerated for up to a week, maybe more. Rewarm before serving.

MINT TISANE

Mint tea is common. Ubiquitous. But old dried packets are faint representations of true mint. They are in stark contrast to this fresh mint tea. Watch the leaves leach their color into the hot water. It's mesmerizing.

Bunches of fresh mint

Hot water

Sugar cubes

Steep the fresh herbs in the hot water. If you like, serve the pot on a tray with a few sugar cubes. Call it the end of your journey into night.

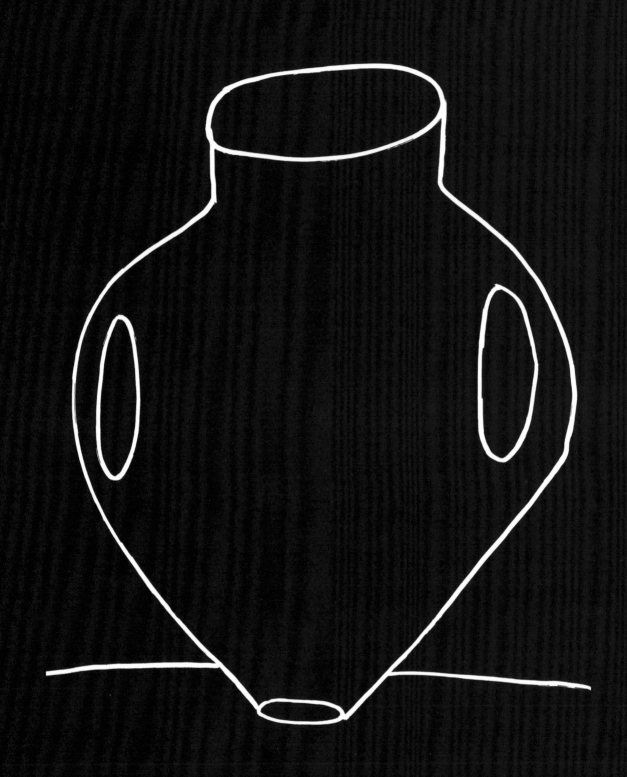

A CLAM
FOR TWELVE

CHOWDER

OYSTERS, BROWN BREAD, & SALTED BUTTER

BEER-BRINED HAM

BOILED POTATOES
with PARSLEY

CROCKED NAVY BEANS & SALT PORK

SOURDOUGH PANCAKES *with* HARD CHEDDAR & APPLE

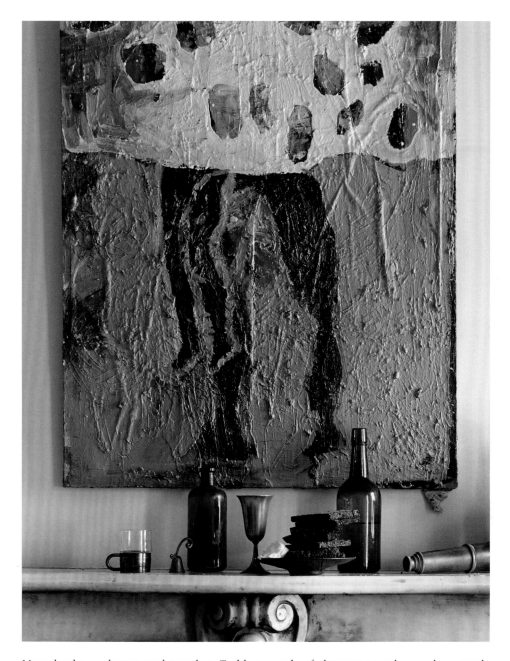

Many books are better read together. Tackle a couple of chapters a week, or, uh, a couple of pages a week. Reward each other with the discussion of subversive themes, bemoan the detailed exploration into the species of whales, delight in a chapter about chowder or two grown men sleeping together with their spears. After *Moby-Dick*, take on *The Odyssey*, the cyclops, the lotus-eaters. Followed by *Crime and Punishment*. Rewrite the night!

This is a series of recipes inspired by Try Pot, the mythical chowder house in Herman Melville's *Moby-Dick*. These are not meant as a menu, instead, perhaps, as just a musing. Consider them recipes that follow in the wake of the book, not each other.

CHOWDER

Two men sharing a clam and a bed. Enough said. Throw everything in the pot and walk away. This pot of stuff is suited for 8 to 10.

"Chowder for breakfast, and chowder for dinner, and chowder for supper, till you began to look for fish-bones coming through your clothes. The area before the house was paved with clam-shells. Mrs. Hussey wore a polished necklace of codfish vertebra; and Hosea Hussey had his account books bound in superior old shark-skin."
—Herman Melville

8 ounces thick-cut bacon, cut into lardons

2 pounds cod, bass, or fluke fillets, cut into manageable portions

Kosher salt and freshly ground pepper

1 pound potatoes, peeled and diced small

2 dozen littleneck clams, scrubbed clean

2 cups heavy cream

2 cups whole milk

4 to 5 tablespoons unsalted butter, cut into cubes

In a large Dutch oven, cook the bacon over medium heat until the fat renders and the bacon is browned, about 10 minutes. With a slotted spoon, remove the bacon from the pot and set aside. Season the fish well with salt and pepper. Place a layer of potatoes on the bottom of the pot, followed by one-third of the fish, one-third of the clams, and a sprinkling of bacon. Continue to layer in such a way until all the ingredients are used. Add the cream and milk; it should just barely cover the other ingredients. You can add a little water, as well, if you don't want the chowder to be so rich. Dot the top with butter, put on the lid, and cook over medium-low heat until the clams open and the potatoes are just tender.

OYSTERS, BROWN BREAD, & SALTED BUTTER

Oysters are often thought of as fine restaurant food, but I think they are more fun to eat at home. They go slower. You appreciate each one. Unlock the shell and toss them into the yard. Enjoy the salt and minerality. Bring the ocean in.

    4 cups heavy cream

    Kosher salt

    4 oysters per person, scrubbed clean

    1 loaf sturdy brown bread, sliced

This is actually just a recipe for butter. In the bowl of a stand mixer, whisk the cream until the fat and whey separate. Listen. The whey will start to slosh around. Churn for a couple minutes more, stopping before the whey cascades out of the bowl. Drape a large sheet of cheesecloth over a large bowl. Pour the butter and whey into the cheesecloth, gather the ends of the cheesecloth, and squeeze the butter to extract as much whey as possible. Really squeeze it hard. Save the whey, as always, for smoothies (see page 62). I like to let the butter drain tied to the faucet, its heavy, yellow mass dripping the occasional cloudy drop of whey into a bowl in the sink. Just let it drain for an hour or so, then return the butter to the bowl, season with salt, and paddle it until combined. Transfer the butter to a crock. Crack open the oysters. Serve with bread.

BEER-BRINED HAM

This brown beer brine will take a week and feed eight. Ideal for a smoker, but if you don't have one, fear not. Any old oven will do.

1½ gallons water

2 pounds kosher salt

1 pound brown sugar

1 teaspoon pink curing salt (sodium nitrate)

3 (12-ounce) bottles of dark beer

4- to 5-pound pork sirloin roast

¼ cup peppercorns, plus additional 2 tablespoons freshly ground

1 bunch thyme

8 bay leaves, crushed

2 tablespoons coriander seeds

2 tablespoons mustard seeds

In a large pot, combine the water, salt, sugar, and pink curing salt, stirring until the sugar and salt dissolves. Add the beer, pork, whole peppercorns, thyme, bay leaves, coriander, and mustard. Refrigerate for 5 days. Remove the pork from the brine, then refrigerate, uncovered, overnight. Discard the brine. The next day, coat it in ground black pepper.

If cooking in a smoker, smoke at low heat 225°F until the ham reaches 180°F, about 4 hours. To cook in an oven, sans smoke, preheat the oven to 350°F. Put the meat in a roasting pan and roast until the ham reaches 180°F, 1½ to 2 hours. Slice and serve or refrigerate until ready to eat.

BOILED POTATOES
with PARSLEY

Everything is unassuming about boiled potatoes, and when they are done with care, they can be a simple pleasure. You want really good, fresh potatoes, often called new potatoes, but any egg-size potato will do. These potatoes are perfect for when your ten guests are suddenly twenty, so always keep extra on hand.

8 tablespoons unsalted butter

4 pounds small new potatoes

Kosher salt

1 bunch parsley, leaves picked

Freshly cracked pepper

Place the butter in a coffee mug on your stove, so it will be near the potato pot. The butter should get a contact high and melt. In a large pot, boil the potatoes in really salty water. Saltier than the sea. The potatoes will float. Simmer them until you can just pass a paring knife through the largest one, about 10 minutes. Drain but don't rinse. A thin film of salt will coat each potato. Place the potatoes in a bowl, then pour the melted butter over them. Coarsely chop the parsley at the last minute, then toss it with the potatoes until evenly coated. Crack lots of pepper over the potatoes and toss again.

CROCKED NAVY BEANS & SALT PORK

Food for months on a ship.

1 onion, diced small

4 cloves garlic, sliced

Olive oil

Kosher salt

3 tablespoons tomato paste

⅓ cup maple syrup

⅓ cup molasses

¼ cup red wine vinegar

3 tablespoons dry mustard powder, we use Coleman's

2 bay leaves

1 pound navy beans, soaked overnight, drained, and rinsed

6 ounces salt pork, thinly sliced

Preheat the oven to 300°F. In a Dutch oven over medium heat, sauté the onions and garlic in oil, seasoned with salt, until they start to sweat. Add the tomato paste and stir to coat the onions. Cook until the onions soften. Add the maple syrup, molasses, vinegar, mustard, and bay leaves. Add the beans and enough water to cover. Bring everything to a boil, then place the salt pork on top of the beans. Cover and bake until the beans are tender, at least 4 hours. The beans will resist softening in the acidic cooking liquid, so keep checking them and add splashes of water as necessary if they start to look dry. Stir occasionally. When the beans are tender, remove from the oven and let them hang out for a bit on the counter. When the beans are warm, not hot, taste and adjust the seasoning. Serve in the pot.

SOURDOUGH PANCAKES *with* HARD CHEDDAR & APPLE

This recipe is inspired by our friend Angela Sherry, who was one of the first servers at Diner. She has a sourdough starter that belonged to her grandfather. She now uses it to make pancakes for her kids. The century-old pancake.

2 tablespoons sourdough starter (see page 256)

2½ cups all-purpose flour

2 cups whole milk, plus more as needed

2 tablespoons butter, plus more for the skillet

2 eggs

¼ cup wheat bran

1 tablespoon sugar

1 teaspoon baking soda

1 teaspoon kosher salt

1 pound sharp cheddar cheese, crumbled

8 apples, cored and thinly sliced

Maple syrup, for serving

In a bowl, stir together the sourdough starter with 2 cups of the flour and the milk. Let sit covered on the counter overnight. It will look really gnarly in the morning, all curdled and weird, but don't fret.

The next morning, make the browned butter. Melt the butter in a pot over low heat, stirring constantly, until the butter is just browned and smells nutty, about 5 minutes. Remove from the heat. Fold the browned butter, along with the eggs, wheat bran, sugar, baking soda, and salt into the starter mixture until just combined. Don't overmix; there will be lumps. If the batter is too thick, thin with a little milk.

In a skillet over medium-low heat, melt 1 teaspoon of butter. Pour ¼ cup of batter into the skillet and cook until bubbles form at the surface, then flip and continue cooking for a minute. Add a teaspoon of butter when the pan seems dry. Transfer to a plate in a low oven while you continue to cook the rest of the pancakes. Crumble the cheddar over each pancake and finish with apples slices and maple syrup.

HOW TO START A STARTER

Mix a cup of flour with a cup of water in a bowl. Let sit uncovered on your kitchen counter overnight. In the morning, discard three-quarters of the starter and mix ¾ cup flour and ¾ cup water into what remains in the bowl. Let the starter sit, uncovered, another night, discarding three-quarters of it and feeding it, again, with equal parts flour and water the next morning. Do this every day for a week. After about a week, your starter should have captured the naturally occurring yeasts and bacteria that float around in its immediate environment. It should start to smell pleasantly sour in the morning after you feed it. It's alive! Observe the natural rise and fall of your starter. It will be affected by heat and humidity, and will change over time. If it ever grows mold, throw it out and start over. You can always *start* over.

ONE GOOD GOOSE

OYSTERS *with*
SHERRY BUTTER

SECOND STOCK

THREE-DAY BRAISE

GOOD FOR THE GANDER

GLAZED CIPOLLINI

DRUNK CABBAGE

TURNIPS & ORANGES

HONEY-POACHED CHESTNUTS

Serves 4 to 6

Only Sean Rembold, the chef of Reynard, could lure me outside to cook goose in the snow. While cooking a whole animal is not always feasible, a whole bird is always a good notion. We chose goose because it carries smoke well. Grill the goose. Grill the oyster. Fire is good all year but better in the winter. Like the whiskey, it will keep you warm.

As much as the perfection of Sean's food seems to point to an obsession, he often reminds me, "It's all about the people." Whether the food is local or organic or grass-fed or butchered in-house, for him it's about who grew it locally, does he share a lively banter with the person, and most important, who is on his team and does he trust, admire, and have fun with them at the end of the night or amid the snow drifts.

OYSTERS *with* SHERRY BUTTER

Arguably, oysters are best left alone, maybe with a drop of lemon juice. But during the winter months, frozen fingers and ice-cold oysters feel incongruous. Instead, build a fire, drink rye outside, and roast oysters until just warm, then anoint with melted butter. If you can't build a fire, the broiler will do.

1 shallot, minced

4 tablespoons unsalted butter

2 tablespoons dry sherry

16 oysters, scrubbed clean

1 lemon, halved

1 handful chervil, chopped

Gloves for eating oysters out of their hot shells

Get your grill good and hot and let the flames die down. In a saucepan over high heat, sauté the shallot with 1 tablespoon of the butter until beginning to brown, about 5 minutes. Lower the heat or move away from the fire so you don't cause a fireball, and add the sherry to the pan, swirling to burn off the booze. Melt the remaining 3 tablespoons butter in the pan. Shuck each oyster. Place the top shells back on. Roast for about 3 minutes on the grill. Keep your gloves on and remove the tops of the oyster shells. Spoon the sherry butter on top, followed by a squeeze of lemon, and a pinch of chervil. Roast for 3 more minutes, until bubbling. Serve with heat warning.

SECOND STOCK

When you source your goose from a local farmer or butcher ask them if they can break it down for you, keeping the breast whole for roasting, legs set aside for braising, the carcass for stock.

1 goose carcass	2 sprigs thyme
3 carrots, snapped in half	2 bay leaves
2 ribs celery	1 teaspoon peppercorns
1 white onion, halved	Kosher salt

Preheat the oven to 350°F. Roast the goose carcass in a roasting pan until golden brown, about an hour. Transfer to a pot with the carrots, celery, onion, thyme, bay leaves, and peppercorns. Season with salt. Add enough cold water to cover and bring to a lively boil. Lower the heat and simmer for 2 hours, skimming the scum that rises to the top diligently. Pour the stock through a strainer lined with cheesecloth set over a large bowl. Discard the solids. Refrigerate in an airtight container until ready to use.

THREE-DAY BRAISE

Goose legs take much longer to cook than the breast. This braise should be prepared ahead of time and rewarmed while the breast is grilling.

Olive oil	Kosher salt
2 goose legs, seasoned with salt the night before	2 ribs celery, halved
	1 carrot, snapped in half
4 cups goose stock (see above)	1 white onion, peeled and halved

In a sauté pan, coated with olive oil and set over medium-high heat, sear the goose legs, skin side down, until golden, about 12 minutes. Pour off the rendered fat and reserve for later. Deglaze the pan by adding the stock and scraping up any browned bits at the bottom. Bring

CONTINUED

the stock to a simmer, then taste and season with salt, if necessary. Add the celery, carrot, and onion, cover the pot, and braise on the stove top, or in a 350°F oven, until the meat can be easily pulled from the bone, about 2 hours. Remove the goose legs from the braise and when cool enough to touch, pick the meat from the bone. Remove the carrot, celery, and onion and discard. Return the goose meat to the braising liquid until ready to use. This can be done up to 3 days in advance. When ready to serve, warm gently in the oven or on the stovetop.

GOOD FOR THE GANDER

Start a fire in a pit with a grate thrown over the top. Not too hot, or the fat on the goose will render and splatter and cause a flare-up to happen. Ease into the fire. Go slow in the snow.

2 goose breasts, wing bones in

Olive oil

Kosher salt

Coarse sea salt

Braised goose legs (page 264)

Rub the goose with olive oil and season well with salt. The breast has a good amount of fat, so it will pick up smoke flavor from the fire. Place the goose breasts skin side down on the grill and cook, rotating 45 degrees every couple of minutes to ensure even cooking. Move the goose to other areas of the grill if the flames rise up too high. Once the fat is nicely rendered and golden brown, flip the breast to the other side. In total, the cooking time should be about 30 minutes. When it's done, the goose breasts should feel plump and taut. The internal temperature should be 140°F. Let the goose breasts rest on a platter, loosely covered with foil, for 10 minutes. Just before serving, carve the breasts and sprinkle a little coarse salt onto the slices. Serve with the braised goose leg.

GLAZED CIPOLLINI

Enlist that friend who asks if you need help to clean the cipollini. Sneaky.

2 pounds cipollini onions, peeled

Olive oil

Kosher salt and freshly ground pepper

4 tablespoons unsalted butter

2 sprigs thyme

½ cup goose stock (page 264), or duck or chicken broth

1 lemon, halved

In a sauté pan over high heat, sear the onions in the oil. Work in batches if all of the onions don't fit in the pan. After a minute or two of undisturbed searing, flip each onion and sear the other side, seasoning well with salt and pepper as you go. Add 2 tablespoons of the butter, the thyme, and a splash of stock. Cover the pan, lower the heat to medium, and steam-roast the onions until just tender, about 5 minutes. Transfer the tender onions to a bowl and continue searing the onions in batches. On the last batch, add the remaining 2 tablespoons butter, the remaining stock, and a squeeze of lemon. Return all of the onions to the pan, lower the heat to medium, and cook until the sauce has reduced to a glaze, about 8 minutes.

DRUNK CABBAGE

3 slices thick-cut bacon, cut into lardons

1 red onion, thinly sliced

1 large red cabbage, thinly sliced

Pinch of sugar

Kosher salt and freshly ground pepper

½ bottle red wine

1 small bunch thyme

2 tablespoons good currant jelly

2 tablespoons unsalted butter

In a heavy, shallow pot, cook the bacon over medium heat until the fat renders and the bacon is browned, about 10 minutes. Add the onion and sauté until translucent. Add the cabbage and sugar, season well with salt and pepper, and stir to get things moving. Turn the heat to high and add the wine to create steam. Add the thyme, stir the cabbage once, then cover and reduce the heat to low. Cook the cabbage for 30 minutes or so, then uncover and cook until the liquid is almost completely reduced, about 30 minutes more. Taste the cabbage, season with salt and pepper if necessary, then fold in the currant jelly and butter.

TURNIPS & ORANGES

12 turnips, scrubbed clean

Olive oil

Kosher salt and freshly ground pepper

1 pound assorted oranges (such as satsuma, clementine, and blood orange)

2 bunches mâche

Juice from ½ lemon

Gruyère cheese, for garnish

Get a grill hot. Let the coals die down to medium. Cut 10 of the turnips into ½-inch-thick wedges. Grill them, dry, turning occasionally to get a nice char but also being careful not to burn them. Once the turnips reach al dente, about 10 minutes, pull them from the grill. Transfer them to a bowl and toss them with a healthy pour of olive oil and season with salt and pepper. Peel the oranges with a knife, being careful to remove as little of the oranges' flesh as possible. Cut off any stray bits of pith, then slice the oranges into ¼-inch rounds. In another bowl, lightly dress the mâche with olive oil and lemon juice. Season with salt and pepper. Thinly slice the remaining 2 turnips with a mandoline over the mâche, then toss together. Arrange the grilled turnips on a platter with the oranges and top with the mâche and raw turnips. With a vegetable peeler, shave ribbons of Gruyère over the top.

HONEY-POACHED CHESTNUTS

Is there a little truth to every cliché? Who can argue with chestnuts in winter?

2 pounds fresh chestnuts

4 cups honey

Blue cheese, for serving

Sliced bread, for serving

Preheat the oven to 425°F. Score by cutting an X into each chestnut. Roast the chestnuts in the oven or over a hot fire until the shells curl, about 30 minutes. Pour the honey into a pot. When the chestnuts are cool enough to touch, start the long, hard road of peeling them. You will get frustrated. It's okay. Enlist another friend to help, probably not the cipollini peeler. Submerge the chestnuts in the honey and cook over very low heat for about an hour. Pull the chestnuts from the honey, reserving the honey for future cocktails. Serve the poached chestnuts with the blue cheese and bread.

THE NIGHT
BEFORE
A NEW YEAR

OR

THE NEW YEAR'S

EVE THAT NEVER

REALLY HAPPENS

OR

THE PAINTED

CLOCK AT 11:59

This is the meal to cap it all off and is inspired by a menu Dave Gould created at Roman's for New Year's Eve. It is fancy and laborious. The pressure is on to be festive that night. It's a good time of year to be ambitious. And in this case, the night is not only about the new year but also about the beginning of our story. That cassoulet, so many years and pages ago.

Time is relative. You'll never find a clock in any of our restaurants. Behind the scenes, we keep time. The countdown. A two-minute fire. A twenty-minute wait for a table. An hour when you're in the weeds flies by in what feels like a minute. A game changer. A cocktail or two. Service has got to be fun. So does New Year's Eve. Since Diner opened, we have celebrated the turning of each year in one of our restaurants, so making this at home was really fun for us. Two New Years? Why not? We cheer to a New Year.

FONDUTA

POLENTA SQUARED

AGNOLOTTI IN BRODO

BRODO

BRAISED BEEF SHANK

RISOTTO MILANESE

A SALAD
BY ANY OTHER NAME

BONET

GOOD NIGHT AMARO

Dinner for 10

FONDUTA

Fontina Val d'Aosta is a particular variety of cheese from Piedmont, Italy. It's used specifically for this recipe, which is like an Italian fondue. Fontina Val d'Aosta melts well, but if you can't find it, any high-quality semisoft raw cow's milk cheese in the style of fontina will do. If you don't have time to make the fried polenta squares, serve the fonduta with fried bread cubes or slices of raw vegetables like fennel and radicchio.

    1 pound Fontina Val d'Aosta cheese

    4 cups whole milk

    ½ cup white wine

    Fried polenta squares, for serving (page 284)

Cut the cheese into cubes. Pour the milk into a large bowl and add the cheese, submerging it in the milk. Cover and refrigerate overnight.

The next day, remove the cheese from the milk. Warm the cheese and wine gently over a double boiler, whisking constantly, until warm and stringy, about 10 minutes. The fonduta should be served immediately, or keep it warm over a flame, like fondue. Serve with fried polenta squares.

POLENTA SQUARED

Polenta can be soft and forgiving, to catch braises and soak up sauces, or depending on the ratio of liquid to ground corn, it can set up firm and dense, as in this recipe. The many textures of polenta.

4 cups water

2 cups whole milk

2 cups coarse-grained polenta

3 tablespoons olive oil

1 tablespoon kosher salt

4 tablespoons unsalted butter

Freshly ground pepper

Neutral oil (such as grapeseed)

Bring the water and milk to a boil in a large saucepan. Whisk in the polenta, oil, and salt. Once large bubbles start to burst at the surface, turn the heat to low and cook very gently, whisking frequently, until the mixture thickens. The polenta will be done when the texture is soft and creamy, and there are no longer any hard, gritty bits. The cooking time can vary, depending on the brand of polenta; it can take up to 3 hours. Keep the flame as low as it can go; stir frequently. When the polenta is soft and creamy, fold in the butter and pepper. Cut the heat, check the seasoning one last time, and pour the polenta onto a baking sheet lined with parchment paper. You are aiming for a 1-inch, even thickness; you may need 2 baking sheets. Refrigerate, uncovered, for 24 hours.

The next day, when the polenta has hardened into a brick, turn it out onto a cutting board. Cut into 1-inch squares. In a sturdy, shallow pot, heat 2 inches of oil until it's 350°F. Working in batches, deep-fry the polenta until golden and crispy, about five minutes. Retrieve squares with a fine-mesh strainer. Drain on paper towels. Serve warm with the fonduta.

AGNOLOTTI IN BRODO

You can make pasta dough on a clean, flat counter, in a bowl, or in a food processor; the manner you make it doesn't really matter. Obviously, pouring an egg into a mound of flour is the most romantic way to make pasta dough, but ultimately, what is most important is the ratio of eggs to flour, which can only be done by and with *feeling*.

2 bunches Swiss chard, stemmed

½ cup ricotta cheese

½ cup grated Parmigiano-Reggiano

½ cup cooked pork sausage, finely chopped

½ cup bread crumbs (page 23)

2 eggs, beaten

½ nutmeg, finely grated

Zest of 1 lemon

Kosher salt and freshly ground pepper

6 cups "00" flour, plus more for dusting

12 egg yolks

6 eggs

1 gallon brodo (page 288)

Juice from 1 lemon

Freshly cracked pepper

To make the filling, in a large pot, boil the Swiss chard in salty water until it loses its bright green color, about 3 minutes. Drain and let cool. Wring out as much water as you can from the leaves, then chop very finely. In a large bowl, stir together the chopped chard with the ricotta, Parmigiano-Reggiano, pork, bread crumbs, eggs, nutmeg, and lemon zest. Season well with salt and ground pepper. Cover and refrigerate until ready to assemble the agnolotti.

To make the pasta dough, mound the flour on a work surface and use your hands to form a well. In a large bowl, whisk together the yolks and eggs. Pour three-quarters of the eggs into the flour and use your fingers to mix it into the flour. Gather a clump of the dough and squeeze it hard in your hand. If it sticks together easily, do not add any more egg. If it sticks together but lots of dry crumbles flake away, add a tiny bit more egg and continue mixing until the dough comes together. This is tough business. You want the dough to be workable but definitely not wet—or soft. It should be firmer than Play-Doh, so be careful to add less of the whisked egg than you think you need. Knead and knead the dough on the counter. Use your muscles. It should feel like work. You will get tired. Once you've worked the dough into a smooth, elastic ball, press your thumb into its surface. It should spring back. If it doesn't, continue kneading for 5 or so more minutes. Tightly cover the dough in plastic wrap and let sit at room temperature for at least 1 hour and up to 3 hours. The dough will soften as it rests and the flour hydrates.

CONTINUED

Line a baking sheet with parchment paper and dust with flour. Clear out your freezer, so there is enough space to store your baking sheet in there. Fill a spray bottle with water. Get a sharp chef's knife or pasta cutter. Cut off one-eighth of the dough ball, tightly covering the remaining dough in plastic wrap as you work. With a rolling pin or a pasta roller, roll out the dough into a long, thin sheet, about $\frac{1}{16}$ inch thick. It should be so thin that you can almost see your hands through the dough. Square off the edges of the pasta sheet with a knife, so you have one long, even rectangle. Cut this rectangle lengthwise into 3-inch strips. Cover all of the strips, except one, with a kitchen towel. Lightly spray the pasta strip with water. With the strip facing you lengthwise, spoon $\frac{1}{2}$-teaspoon drops of filling along the length of the strip, spaced 1 inch apart, running down the center of the strip. Fold the edge closest to you up over the filling, and press it down, leaving a $\frac{1}{2}$-inch strip of dough bare along the top edge. Press the pasta between each drop of filling to seal, pinching around the filling to press out any air pockets. Run your pasta cutter across the top of the bare dough. Roll the length of the entire strip over, so the filling is now fully encapsulated with the remaining $\frac{1}{2}$-inch strip of bare dough. This will create the pocket effect.

Now, secure the length of pasta with your left hand and put a pasta cutter in your right hand. Cut each agnolotti vertically, as close as you can to the filling, without breaking the seal. When you cut forward, roll the the agnolotti over itself. This will form its characteristic agnolotti shape, like an envelope. Roll the cutter firmly and forcefully, to help the edges seal. Transfer the agnolotti to the prepared baking sheet in a single layer and freeze. Continue to roll out the pasta dough and form the agnolotti until you run out of dough or filling. Freeze until ready to cook. Will keep for up to 4 or 5 days.

On the day you want to serve the agnolotti in brodo, bring the brodo to a low simmer in a large pot. Check the seasoning and add more salt if necessary. Bring a large pot of water to a boil. Drop the agnolotti into the boiling water, just a dunk to remove their coats of flour, then transfer them with a fine-mesh strainer to the brodo. Cook the agnolotti in the brodo until just tender, 6 to 8 minutes. When ready to serve, ladle a cup of brodo and about 8 agnolottis into bowls, sprinkling a few drops of lemon juice and a pinch of cracked pepper over each bowl.

BRODO

Make this brodo one night, a week before New Year's Eve, or one night every week, all winter long. In truth, you could just serve this and forget the agnolotti and risotto. This will make about a gallon of broth but can easily be doubled, even tripled. For this menu you'll need a gallon and a half, so double this recipe and freeze whatever you have left. It's nice to have a little extra on hand, perfect hot in a coffee mug for those who need a little steadying on the first day of the year.

1 large capon or chicken

2 pounds beef marrowbones

⅓ pound prosciutto, cubed

2 ribs celery, snapped in half

1 carrot

1 leek, cleaned

Handful of dried porcini mushrooms

2 cloves garlic, peeled

¼ cinnamon stick

For this brodo, we chose a capon for its rich flavor and golden fat. Place the capon in a large pot, add enough cold water to cover, and bring to a boil. Lower the heat and simmer for 2 hours, skimming diligently. Add the marrowbones, prosciutto, celery, carrot, leek, mushrooms, garlic, and cinnamon and cook for 1 hour more. Skim diligently. Strain through a fine-mesh sieve lined with cheesecloth, set over a large bowl. Discard the solids. Cover and refrigerate until ready to use.

BRAISED BEEF SHANK

Piennolo tomatoes are a grape tomato, grown in the lava-rich soils of Mount Vesuvius. They remain delicate and sweet when preserved and can be found in specialty food shops. If unavailable, look for San Marzano or another Italian variety.

6 pounds beef shank, cut into 2-inch-thick pieces

Kosher salt

Olive oil

2 ribs celery, chopped

1 large white onion, chopped

1 large carrot, chopped

½ cup anchovy fillets

Handful of fresh sage

Handful of dried porcini mushrooms

½ bottle red wine

2 cups Piennolo tomatoes or any slightly sweet preserved Italian tomato

Risotto Milanese (page 295), for serving

Season the beef well with salt, ideally the day before you want to serve it. The next day, in a wide, heavy-bottomed pot over medium heat, gently browning the beef in oil, working in batches. Add more oil as needed. This will take about 30 minutes. Add the celery, onion, carrot, anchovies, sage, and porcini and cook until softened and slightly caramelized, about 8 minutes. Deglaze the pan by adding the wine and scraping up any browned bits at the bottom of the pot. Add the tomatoes and two cups of water and bring to a boil.

Preheat the oven to 300°F. Taste the braising liquid and season with salt, if necessary. Return the beef to the pot, cover, and braise in the oven until the meat is tender but not falling off the bone, 3 to 5 hours. When finished, cut the heat and let rest for an hour or two at room temperature or cover and refrigerate overnight. When ready to serve, warm over low heat and serve with the risotto.

RISOTTO MILANESE

1 white onion, diced

Large pinch of saffron

7 tablespoons unsalted butter

4 cups Arborio rice

½ cup white wine

8 cups brodo (page 288)

½ cup grated Parmigiano-Reggiano

Braised Beef Shank (page 293)

Freshly ground pepper

In a large saucepan over medium heat, gently cook the onion and saffron in 4 tablespoons of butter until the onion is soft, about 5 minutes. Add the rice and cook until you hear crackling sounds from the rice. Deglaze the pan by adding the wine and scraping up any browned bits at the bottom of the pan. Add 1 cup of the brodo and simmer the risotto gently until all of the brodo has been absorbed. Add another cup, continue to simmer, stirring occasionally, until the brodo is absorbed. Gentle cooking is more important than constant simmering. In total, the rice should absorb around 8 cups of brodo, this will take 20 to 25 minutes. The rice should be tender but still have a bit of chew to it. Cut the heat and let the risotto rest for a minute or two. A literal minute or two. Fold the remaining 3 tablespoons of butter and the Parmigiano-Reggiano into the rice. Taste and adjust the seasoning. To serve, pour the risotto onto a platter and spoon the braised beef shank over it. Finish with black pepper.

A SALAD
BY ANY OTHER NAME

This salad is a balancing act between bitter greens and the sweet pop of persimmon.

2 heads radicchio, leaves torn

2 heads escarole, leaves picked

3 bulbs fennel, thinly sliced

1 red onion, thinly sliced

Juice of 2 lemons

Olive oil

Kosher salt

6 Fuyu persimmons, peeled and thinly sliced

Seeds of 2 pomegranates

In the largest bowl you have, toss together the radicchio, escarole, fennel, onion, lemon juice, oil, and salt. Taste a leaf and adjust the seasoning, if necessary. Add the persimmons and pomegranate seeds, and toss together again.

BONET

Basically, cookies and cream, bonet is an age-old recipe from the Piedmont region of Italy. You will need two flameproof 9-inch baking dishes for this recipe.

6 oranges

1½ cups sugar

1 cup sugar plus 5½ tablespoons

1 cup whole milk

1 cup heavy cream

30 amaretti cookies
(about 160 grams), finely crumbled

4 eggs

2 tablespoons Dutch-processed cocoa powder

2 shots of espresso

2 tablespoons dark rum

Dark chocolate

Hazelnuts

To make the candied orange peel, cut the top and bottom off the oranges so they can sit flat, then peel the oranges with a knife, removing as little of the white pith as possible. Thinly slice the peels into ⅙-inch strips. Bring a pot of water to a boil. Add the orange peels and blanch them until tender, 6 to 8 minutes. Drain well. In a medium saucepan, bring 1¼ cups of the sugar and 1 cup water to a boil. Add the blanched peels and simmer until translucent, about 10 minutes. Remove the peels with a slotted spoon and let drain on a wire rack set over a baking sheet, separating the peels so they don't stick together. Let dry for 2 hours, then toss with the remaining ¼ cup sugar in a bowl. Let dry on a baking sheet lined with parchment paper overnight.

To make the bonet, sprinkle ½ cup of the sugar over the bottom of a flameproof 9-inch baking dish. Cook over medium heat until the sugar caramelizes to a deep mahogany color, about 3 minutes. Cut the heat and set aside to cool. Repeat with another flameproof 9-inch baking dish and ½ cup sugar.

Preheat the oven to 300°F. In a saucepan over medium heat, warm the milk, cream, and amaretti. Meanwhile, whisk together the eggs, remaining 5½ tablespoons sugar, the cocoa, espresso, and rum in a small bowl. Add a splash of the warm milk mixture to the egg mixture, then slowly incorporate the tempered egg mixture into the warm milk mixture. Pour the custard into the baking dishes. Place the dishes in a pan, or 2 separate pans if need be, and pour hot water into the pan to at half way up the height of the custard dish. Bake, uncovered, in the hot water bath until set, about 30 minutes. Let cool to room temperature. You can serve the bonets in their dishes or invert them onto plates, if you like drama. To unmold a bonet, place a flat serving plate over the top of the bonet's baking dish. With a firm grasp and full confidence, flip the dish over quickly. The bonet will unmold and settle onto the serving plate. Serve with the dark chocolate, hazelnuts, and candied orange peels.

GOOD NIGHT AMARO

Cleanup is the true moment of togetherness. Washing dishes. Tossing napkins into a pile on the floor. Packing up. Caring for the food that's left behind. Saying goodnight. Goodnight, balloons that are losing their spunk. Good night, wine-stained tablecloth. Good night, deep-soaking pots.

After all of that, ease into the darkness with a glass of amaro. A spirit like no other. It's hard to say good-bye. It's hard to close a restaurant down at the end of the night. It's hard when dinner comes to an end. It's hard to end the book. It's hard to say goodnight to the amaro. It's hard to say goodnight to the light.

MANY THANKS TO

KATE HULING for love

CAROLINE FIDANZA for always knowing what to do

MARK FIRTH for making it fun

SEAN REMBOLD for making it the funniest

DAVE GOULD for being a classic

KEN WISS for all the cool

JASON SCHWARTZ for riding bikes

TOM BUDNY for making it elegant

JOHN CONNOLLY for making it happen

MARISA MARTHALLER for style and grace

RUSTUN & MICHELLE NICHOLS for leaving a lasting impression

AUSTIN HALL for waking up so early

SCARLETT LINDEMAN for knowing about everything

LEAH CAMPBELL for taking care of every single thing

JULIA GILLARD for the point of view

BECKY JOHNSON for your touch

LARS KARLSSON for all the solutions

NEALE HOLADAY for being sweet and savory

GUY GREENBERG for taking names

LEE CAMPBELL for her good taste

LEE DESROSIERS for always showing up

DEANNA BENOR for running numbers

MIKE FADEM for shepherding

SUSAN THOMPSON for heavy lifting

LISA KIM for friendship

JAMES O'BOYLE for taking care of business

MARIE TRIBOUILLOY for talking cocktails

JOSH WILES for the music and the spirits in the night

RYAN SEATON for the daily

SHANE FEIRSTEIN for the head start

JIM MCHUGH & KATIE EASTBURN for changing the game

ANGELA SHERRY for pancakes

ALEKSEY & JULIET KRAVCHUK for the light

PETER LAWRENCE & JED WALENTAS for being my partners

MILLICENT SOURIS for telling all

SVEN DELVECCHIO for telling everyone

EVAN DUNN for doing what his sister tells him

PETER MILNE GREINER for always writing

EMMA MANNHEIMMER for helping in every way

ALEJANDRO CHAMPION for the mezcal

KATY PORTE for being built like light

ELIJAH for the magic, BÉA for the social grace, ROMAN for positivity,

PALOMA for sheer will

Thank you to our Mothers and Fathers and Stepparents, Sisters and Brothers,

In-laws and Outlaws

KATHERINE COWLES for the prompt

NIKOLE HERRIOTT for the comma

MICHAEL GRAYDON for the cinema

JENNY WAPNER & TEN SPEED PRESS for the freedom and the structure

AMY WILSON for making it look good

NINA LALLI for picking up all of the pieces we almost dropped

ANDREW KATZOWITZ for holding the light

CERISE MAYO for problem solving

EVERYONE at LDM

PATTY GENTRY for the love of vegetables

ISABELLA ROSSELLINI for the set

GUY JONES for wisdom and the Molson

HENRY & CASEY AND THE WHOLE AMISH CREW for farming with mules

LEE & GEORGIA AND THE WHOLE KINDERHOOK CREW for growing the grass

RICHARD for being the lucky dog of the bunch

—

MANY THANKS TO

ALSO:

TJ BURNHAM

KEN AND JASMINE REYNOLDS

YESSENIA SANTIBANEZ

SERGIO GARCIA

SARAH GASKINS

TOM MYLAN & ANNALIESE GRIFFIN

BRENT YOUNG

MICHAEL MANGIERE

FRANK REED

ROSS GARCIA

BEN JACKSON

JUAN RODRIGUEZ

POLIN BAEZ

MICHAEL KALE

STEPHANIE REAGOR

ELIZABETH SCHULA

REBECCA COLLERTON

DERICK HOLT

KIRSTEN FAZZARI

JOHN HALE

AARON CROWDER

ERIN KANAGY-LOUX

CHRISTINA BARONE

SHANNON PRITCHETT

BRUCE SPRINGSTEEN

HERMÈS

Thank you BIRD

Thank you ANNA for the poetry

Thank you ANDREW for the magic

Thank you all the servers, all the bartenders, all the cooks, all the porters,

all the managers, all the guests, all the animals, all the vegetables, all the minerals,

all the farmers, all the winemakers, all the writers, and all the artists. Thank you all the

makers and doers. We could go on and on but we can't go on without you.

Thank you all.

—

MANY THANKS TO

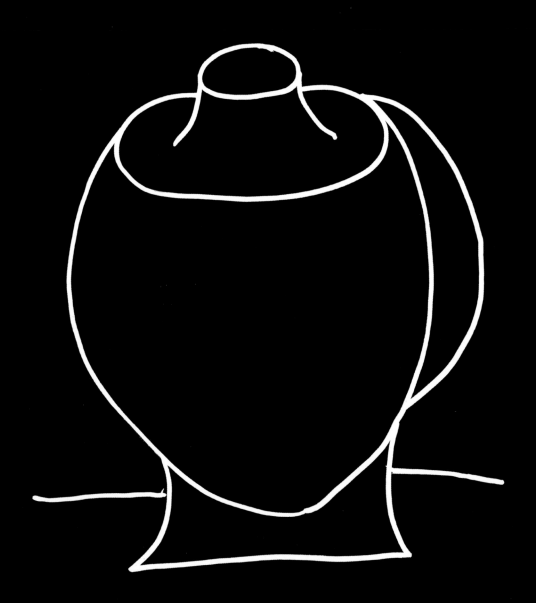

INDEX

ALL RIGHTS RESERVED.
PUBLISHED IN THE UNITED STATES BY TEN SPEED PRESS, AN
IMPRINT OF THE CROWN PUBLISHING GROUP, A DIVISION OF
PENGUIN RANDOM HOUSE LLC, NEW YORK.
WWW.CROWNPUBLISHING.COM
WWW.TENSPEED.COM

TEN SPEED PRESS AND THE TEN SPEED PRESS COLOPHON ARE
REGISTERED TRADEMARKS OF PENGUIN RANDOM HOUSE LLC.

LIBRARY OF CONGRESS CATALOGING-IN-PUBLICATION DATA

CIP DATA ON FILE WITH THE PUBLISHER

HARDCOVER ISBN: 978-1-60774-846-5
EBOOK ISBN: 978-1-60774-847-2

PRINTED IN CHINA

DESIGN BY BECKY JOHNSON
PROP STYLIST AMY WILSON

10 9 8 7 6 5 4 3 2 1

FIRST EDITION